Crafty Dolls
Jane Bull

DK

This book is for...

...my husband Stephen and our three children...

Lottie, Billy, and Jim

Hello, I'm
Jane Bull.

Hello, I'm
Jane Bull.

Welcome to Crafty Dolls

Why not make a doll that looks just like you
or someone you know? How can you resist?
This book is full of ideas to get
you started. Have fun!

LONDON, NEW YORK, MUNICH,
MELBOURNE, and DELHI

DESIGN AND TEXT Jane Bull
PHOTOGRAPHER Andy Crawford
SENIOR EDITOR Carrie Love
DESIGNERS Charlotte Johnson, Hannah Moore
JACKET DESIGNERS Rosie Levine
and Ria Holland
PRODUCTION EDITOR Andy Hilliard
PRODUCTION CONTROLLER Ché Creasey
MANAGING EDITOR Penny Smith
MANAGING ART EDITOR Marianne Markham
CREATIVE DIRECTOR Jane Bull
CATEGORY PUBLISHER Mary Ling

First published in Great Britain in 2014 by
Dorling Kindersley Limited
80 Strand, London WC2R 0RL
A Penguin Random House Company

10 9 8 7 6 5 4 3 2 1
001–192952–07/14
Copyright © 2014 Dorling Kindersley Limited
Copyright © 2014 Jane Bull

A CIP catalogue record for this book
is available from the British Library.

ISBN: 978-1-40934-646-3

Printed and bound in China
by South China Printing Co. Ltd.

Discover more at
www.dk.com

Meet the dolls

You'll need the sewing kit and other essentials for every project. See page 112.

Lottie

Rag dolls

Lottie dolls

One pattern, lots of dolls - here's a simple rag-doll design that can be adapted to make all kinds of characters.

Doll templates and "how-to"

The templates for making the dolls can be found on pages 14–15, including those for the body, hair, shoes and some clothes. Additional templates can be found with dolls such as Shelly the mermaid and Cinders. The steps for making the dolls are on pages 16–19.

How to begin your doll

1 Use the templates on pages 14–15.

For the body, fold a piece of tracing paper in half.

Place the paper over the shape and draw around the outline.

2 Keeping the paper folded, cut out the shape.

For other shapes, use a single layer of paper and simply follow the lines.

Open up the paper, ready for pinning to the fabric.

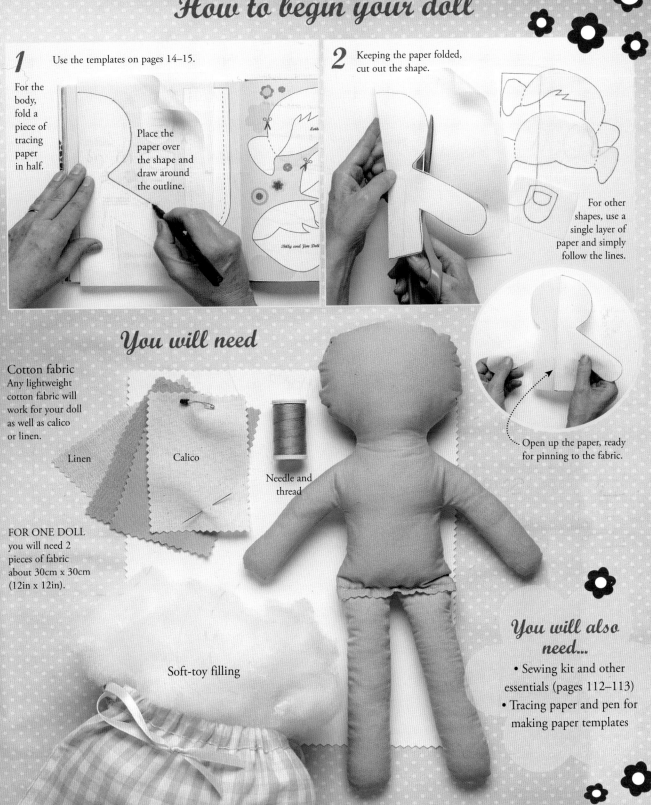

You will need

Cotton fabric
Any lightweight cotton fabric will work for your doll as well as calico or linen.

Linen

Calico

Needle and thread

FOR ONE DOLL you will need 2 pieces of fabric about 30cm x 30cm (12in x 12in).

Soft-toy filling

You will also need...

• Sewing kit and other essentials (pages 112–113)
• Tracing paper and pen for making paper templates

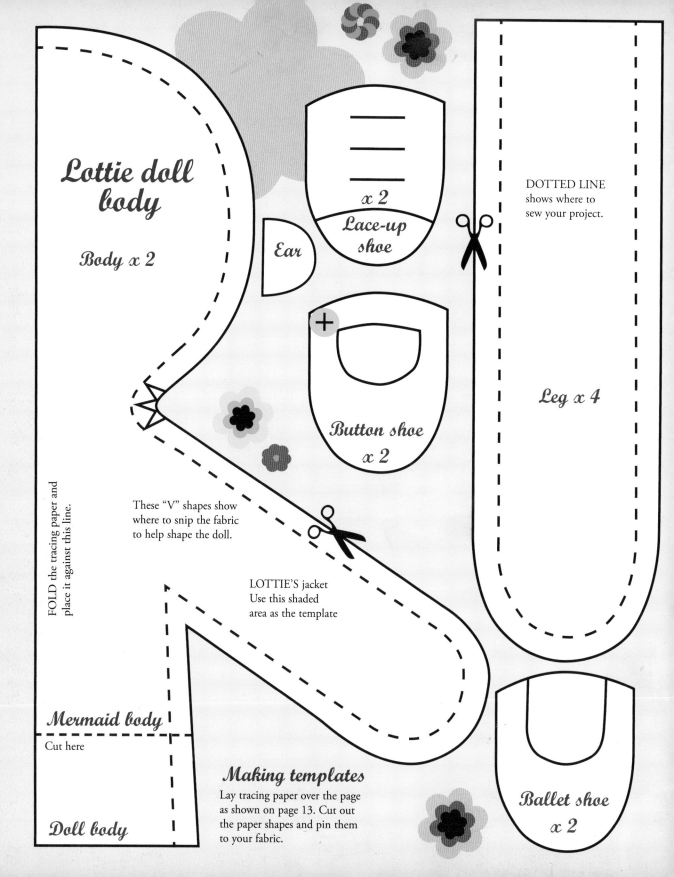

Lottie doll body

Body x 2

Ear

x 2
Lace-up shoe

DOTTED LINE shows where to sew your project.

Leg x 4

Button shoe x 2

These "V" shapes show where to snip the fabric to help shape the doll.

FOLD the tracing paper and place it against this line.

LOTTIE'S jacket Use this shaded area as the template

Mermaid body

Cut here

Doll body

Making templates
Lay tracing paper over the page as shown on page 13. Cut out the paper shapes and pin them to your fabric.

Ballet shoe x 2

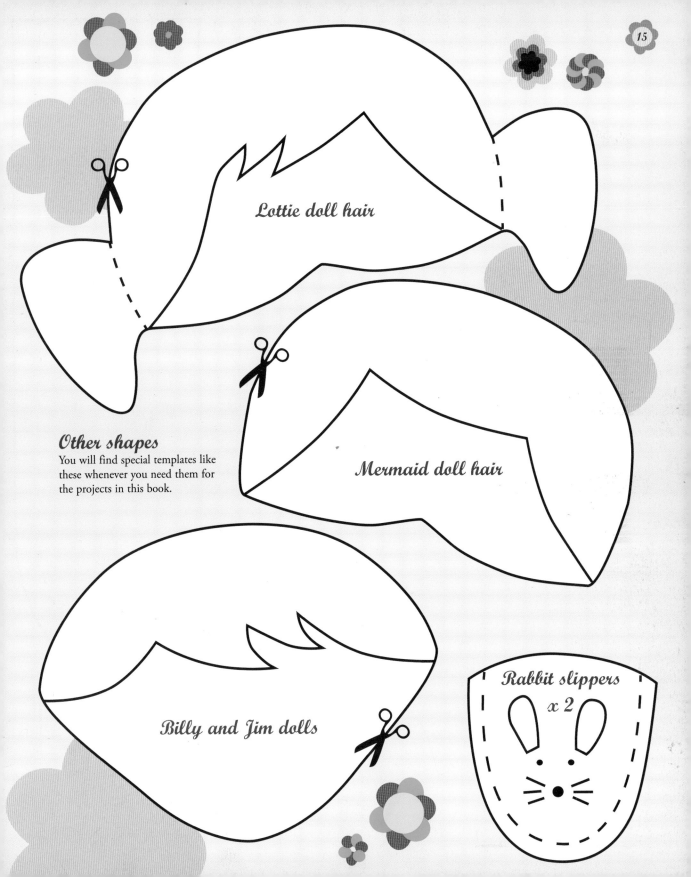

Lottie doll hair

Mermaid doll hair

Other shapes
You will find special templates like these whenever you need them for the projects in this book.

Billy and Jim dolls

Rabbit slippers
x 2

How to make a Lottie doll

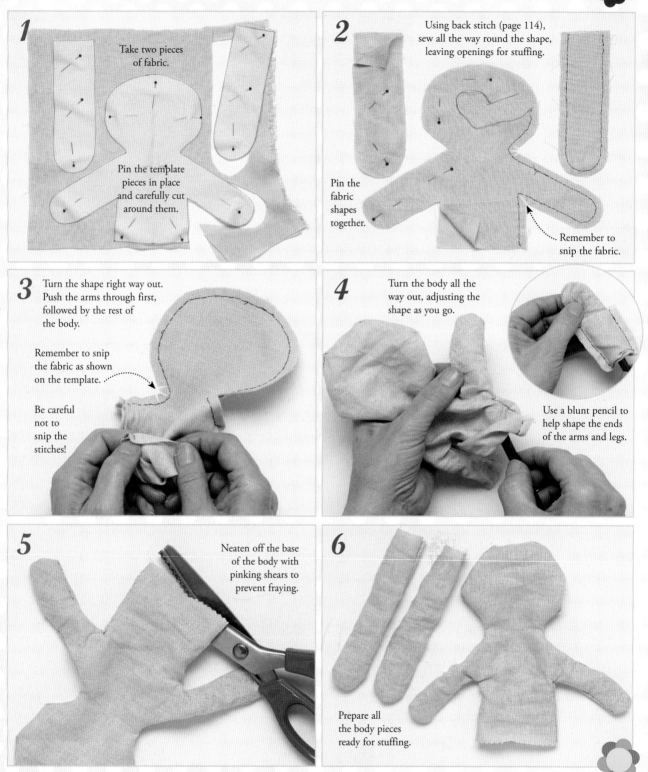

1 Take two pieces of fabric.

Pin the template pieces in place and carefully cut around them.

2 Using back stitch (page 114), sew all the way round the shape, leaving openings for stuffing.

Pin the fabric shapes together.

Remember to snip the fabric.

3 Turn the shape right way out. Push the arms through first, followed by the rest of the body.

Remember to snip the fabric as shown on the template.

Be careful not to snip the stitches!

4 Turn the body all the way out, adjusting the shape as you go.

Use a blunt pencil to help shape the ends of the arms and legs.

5 Neaten off the base of the body with pinking shears to prevent fraying.

6 Prepare all the body pieces ready for stuffing.

7 Fill the body and legs, putting small clumps of stuffing in at a time.

Keep adding stuffing, working it into the shape with your fingers.

8 Work the stuffing into all the corners to make the body firm, but not overstuffed.

Use a blunt pencil to help shape the arms and legs.

9

All the parts are ready to assemble. Don't over fill, as this will make it difficult to attach the legs.

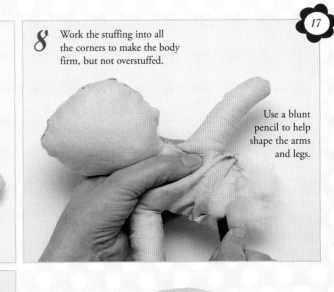

I'm ready!

This is the basic Lottie doll ready to be transformed how ever you choose.

10

Sew the ends of the legs together to make it easier to attach to the body.

11

Pin the legs inside the base of the body and sew securely in place.

NOTE: The body for Shelly the mermaid is cut shorter than the Lottie doll.

Making hair and faces

Each of your dolls can have different colour hair in whatever style you choose. Here's how to make the hair and attach it to the doll's head. For the face, pencil in the features then sew over the marks.

You will need

• Sewing kit (pages 112–113)
FOR HAIR • Felt fabric
FOR FEATURES
• Embroidery thread • Pencil

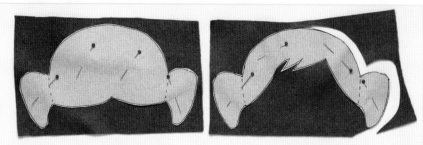

Trace out the patterns for the hair and pin them to the felt fabric.

Cut out the hair shapes.

1

Pin the pieces together and over stitch the edges.

Use running stitch here. ......

2

Continue stitching around the bunches. ...

3

Fit the hair onto the head.

Adjust the hair until it fits snugly onto the head and is in the right position.

4

Sew the hair onto the head all the way round the back.

Make a face

1 Lightly pencil on the eyes, nose, and mouth.

2 Knot the end of the thread and put the needle in through the side of the head.

Bring the needle out at the front and sew a few stitches to make the eye shape.

Bring the needle back out at the side of the head, cut off the thread and the knot.

3 For the mouth and nose make small stitches and repeat the steps shown above.

Give her ribbons on her bunches made from small pieces of felt (see page 20). Cut them out and stitch in position.

Making faces

Getting a cute faces, isn't easy – are the eyes too high or too far apart? So experiment. Lightly pencil in the eyes and mouth before you begin sewing.

Add some ears   See the Billy and Jim dolls on page 24.

Cut out the ear shapes using the template on page 14.

Position the ear against the head seam and over stitch it neatly to the head.

Repeat this for the other ear.

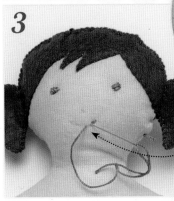

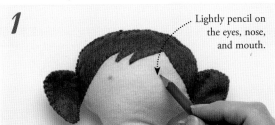

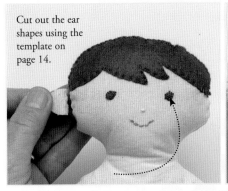

Lottie doll

Lottie loves craft – with her scissors in hand and her knitting needles at the ready, she's set to get crafty. She's a crafty doll herself – with this basic design you can make all kinds of other characters.

What a doll!

Here Lottie is all dressed up for a summer's day, in a matching blouse and skirt, a fitted felt jacket, and a cute little pair of felt shoes.

Find the template for the Lottie doll on pages 13–19

Lottie's summer clothes

See the next page for how to make the clothes .

Red felt ribbons

Felt jacket

Made up of three pieces of felt from the template on page 14.

Blouse and shirt

These two items are in matching lightweight cotton. The skirt is gathered up simply with a ribbon and tied at the waist.

Decorate the skirt with ribbons like this rickrack

Add tiny felt buttons with a cross stitch.

Felt shoes

You will need

A BASIC DOLL (pages 13–19) • Sewing kit (pages 112–113)
SKIRT and BLOUSE: Cotton fabric
45cm x 25cm (18in x 10in) • Ribbon 40cm (16in) • Rickrack for trimming
JACKET: Felt 2 pieces 23cm x 12cm (9in x 4½in)
SHOES: Felt scraps for shoes and buttons

How to make Lottie's clothes

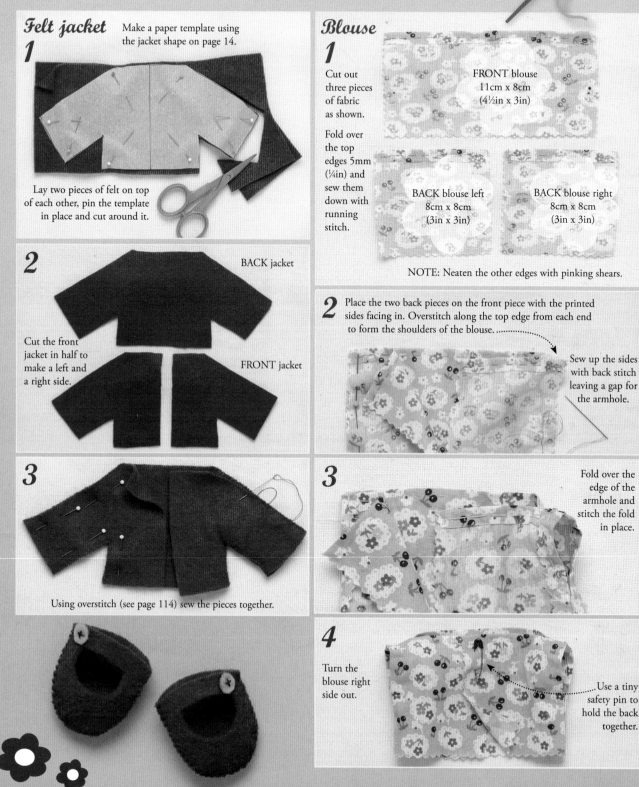

Felt jacket

1 Make a paper template using the jacket shape on page 14.

Lay two pieces of felt on top of each other, pin the template in place and cut around it.

2 Cut the front jacket in half to make a left and a right side.

BACK jacket

FRONT jacket

3 Using overstitch (see page 114) sew the pieces together.

Blouse

1 Cut out three pieces of fabric as shown.

Fold over the top edges 5mm (¼in) and sew them down with running stitch.

FRONT blouse
11cm x 8cm
(4½in x 3in)

BACK blouse left
8cm x 8cm
(3in x 3in)

BACK blouse right
8cm x 8cm
(3in x 3in)

NOTE: Neaten the other edges with pinking shears.

2 Place the two back pieces on the front piece with the printed sides facing in. Overstitch along the top edge from each end to form the shoulders of the blouse.

Sew up the sides with back stitch leaving a gap for the armhole.

3 Fold over the edge of the armhole and stitch the fold in place.

4 Turn the blouse right side out.

Use a tiny safety pin to hold the back together.

Shoes x 2

Trace out the shoe template on paper and pin it to the felt.

To add a button cut out a small disc of felt

Stitch the front and back pieces together using overstitch.

Attach it to the shoe with a cross stitch.

Handy tip

Pinking shears – to save you having to neaten every edge of fabric, simply use pinking shears to stop the sides from fraying and for a decorative effect as well.

Skirt

1 Cut a piece of fabric 30cm x 10cm (12in x 4in).

Fold down the top edge 1.5cm (⅝in).

Sew the edge down using running stitch.

Turn up the hem 1.5cm (⅝in).

Stitch rickrack to the front of the skirt along the hem edge. Use pinking shears to neaten the edge of the fabric.

2 Cut a piece of ribbon 25cm (10in) and fasten a safety pin to one end.

Push the pin into the gap in the fabric and work it along.

Fit the skirt around your doll's waist and tie the ribbon into a bow.

3 Pull the pin out at the other end. Don't pull the ribbon all the way through.

Gather up the fabric on the ribbon.

Lottie's brothers

Lottie has two brothers, Billy and Jim. These boys are made from the Lottie doll pattern too, but they have short neat hair and little ears.

Find the template
for Lottie doll on pages 13–19

Jim   Lottie   Billy

Jim's jumper and jeans

See the next page for how to make the clothes.

Jumper

Knitted in four pieces in stocking stitch. Stripes knitted in to create a pattern.

Jeans

Made in a lightweight cotton fabric that looks like denim.

Satchel

Shoulder bag made from felt with felt straps.

Shoes

Contrasting felt for the uppers, the soles, and the toes. Finished off with a lacing effect.

You will need

A BASIC DOLL (pages 13–19) • Sewing kit (pages 112–113)
SWEATER: Ball of wool for the main colour, scraps for stripes
JEANS: Cotton fabric 15cm x 22cm (6in x 9in), elastic 18cm (7in)
SHOES and BAG: Scraps of felt in red, grey, white, two browns

How to make jeans

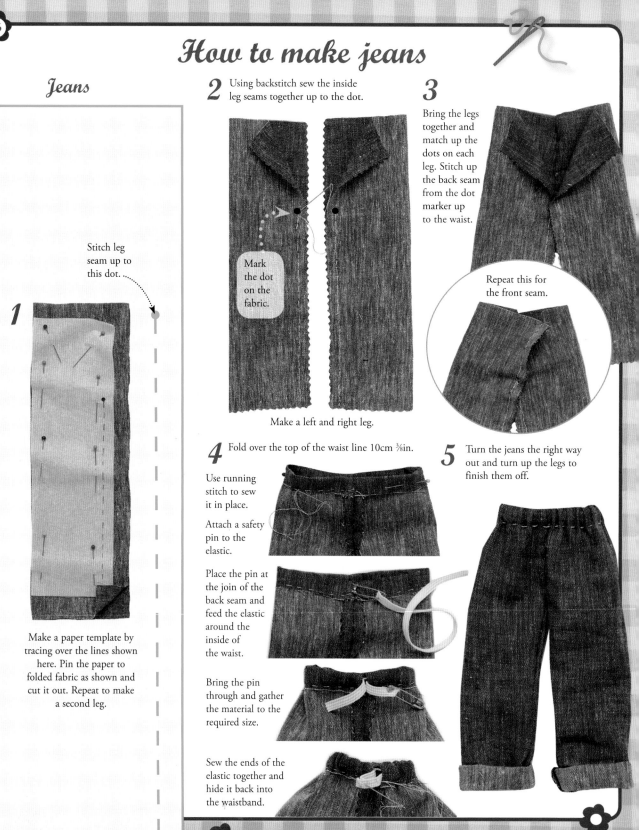

Jeans

FOLD LINE for FABRIC

1

Stitch leg seam up to this dot. ....

Make a paper template by tracing over the lines shown here. Pin the paper to folded fabric as shown and cut it out. Repeat to make a second leg.

2
Using backstitch sew the inside leg seams together up to the dot.

Mark the dot on the fabric.

Make a left and right leg.

3
Bring the legs together and match up the dots on each leg. Stitch up the back seam from the dot marker up to the waist.

Repeat this for the front seam.

4
Fold over the top of the waist line 10cm ⅜in.

Use running stitch to sew it in place.

Attach a safety pin to the elastic.

Place the pin at the join of the back seam and feed the elastic around the inside of the waist.

Bring the pin through and gather the material to the required size.

Sew the ends of the elastic together and hide it back into the waistband.

5
Turn the jeans the right way out and turn up the legs to finish them off.

Sweater

FRONT and BACK
Use stocking stitch.
Cast on 24 stitches.
Rib 6 rows: Row 1: knit 1,
purl 1, repeat to end.
Repeat row 1 five more times.
Work 21 rows in stocking stitch
beginning with a knit row.
Rib 3 rows: Row 1: knit 1, Purl 1,
repeat to end. Repeat row 1 two
more times. Cast off.

SLEEVES x 2
Use stocking stitch.
Cast on 20 stitches.
Rib 3 rows: Row 1: knit 1,
purl 1, repeat to end.
Row 2 and 3: repeat row 1.
Work 11 rows in stocking stitch
beginning with a knit row.
Cast off.

3 rows of ribbing

6 rows of ribbing

3 rows of ribbing

1 Place the front and back pieces right sides down.

Stitch along the edges each side to create the neck line.

TIP: Use the loose ends to sew up the edges.

2 Align the centre of the sleeve with the neckline and pin the edges together.

Sew the edges together to attach the sleeve to the front and back pieces.

Open the knitting out flat

3 Fold the knitting over with the reverse side out.

Sew the edges together up the sides and along the sleeves.

Turn the finished sweater right side out and pop it on.

Sweater designs
You can change this sweater pattern to create other designs, including stripes, bands, and multicoloured yarn for an instant colourful effect.

Shoes x 2
Trace the shoe templates onto paper and pin them to the felt.

Decorate the front first - sew on the toecap and add the laces

Using overstitch sew the front and back together.

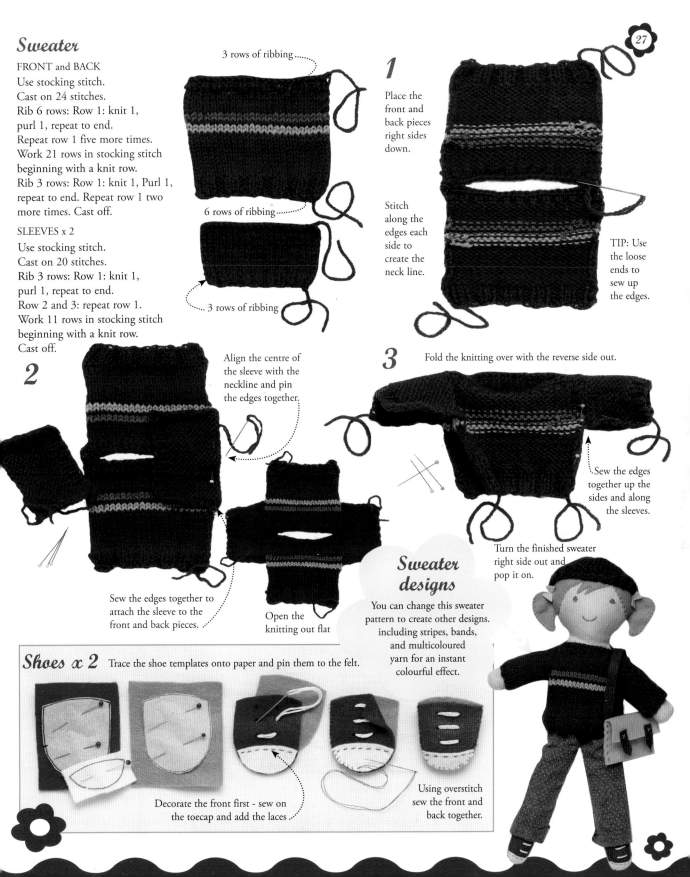

Lottie, Billy and...

Lottie

Billy

24

Make Lottie's jumper using the pattern for Jim's. Use multi-coloured yarn to create the pattern.

Lottie's jeans are just the same as Jim's but hers are made from spotty lightweight cotton fabric.

Bill's sweater is also made using the knitting pattern. Make this two-colour effect by knitting half way up in dark blue and changing to pale blue for the top half and arms.

Here they are, ready to go out and about - Billy with his camera set

...Jim

Jim

Meow
MEOW!

Jim's beany hat is simple
to do – just knit a
rectangle shape, sew the
sides together, then
gather it up at the top.

For his scarf, simply
make a length of knitting
long enough to wrap
round his neck.
See pages 32-33

Woof
WOOF!

to take some snaps and Jim with his dog, who's just spied the cat in the window...!

Make accessories for your dolls

Beanie hats

Multi-coloured yarn gives a stripy effect.

Woolly scarf

Shoulder bags

Make bags in different colours to match outfits.

Camera

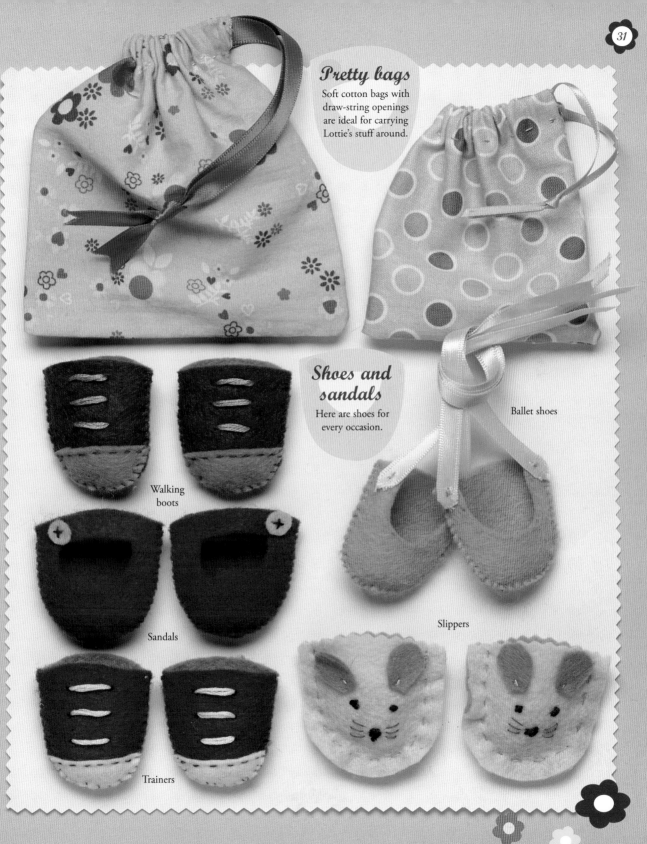

Pretty bags
Soft cotton bags with draw-string openings are ideal for carrying Lottie's stuff around.

Shoes and sandals
Here are shoes for every occasion.

Ballet shoes

Walking boots

Sandals

Slippers

Trainers

How to make accessories

Camera

Black yarn for strap

Scraps of black and grey felt

Cut out felt shapes.

For front and back 2.5cm x 4cm (1in x 1½in)

6mm x 4cm (¼in x 1½in) strips for decoration and small discs for lens

Sew all the shapes in place on the front of the camera.

Sew the front camera piece to the back.

Stitch the end of the yarn to the back of the camera.

Woolly scarf

Cast on more stitches to make a wider scarf.

Cast on 8 stitches. In knit stitch, work rows until the scarf is as long as you want it.

Shoe bag

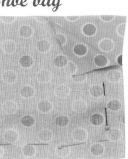

Cut a piece of fabric 17cm (6¾in) x 10 cm (4in) and fold it in half right sides together.

Pin along the base and side. Stitch together.

Fold over the top edge 12mm (½in), pin, and stitch.

Pull the ribbon through the fold using a safety pin attached to the end.

Turn the bag right side out. Pull the ribbon to gather up the opening.

Beanie hat

Cast on 48 stitches.
Rib stitch 5 rows.
Row 1: knit 1,
purl 1 to end.
Repeat 4 more rows.
Work 10 rows in
stocking stitch.
Cast off.

Pull the yarn to gather
up the knitting. Secure
the yarn to finish.

Fold the work
in half, right
sides together.

Stitch side
seam together.

Stitch around the top
edge of the knitting.

Satchel bag

Cut out the felt.
Buckle straps:
12mm x 4cm
(½in x 1½in).
Bag straps:
12mm x 11.5cm
(½in x 4½in)
and 12mm x
7.5cm (½in x
3in).

Felt for the bag
8cm x 18cm
(3⅛in x 7in)

Fold
over the
bottom
third of
the felt.

Stitch in
place.

Sew the
straps
together.

Attach the
buckle straps
to the front
of the
bag and
stitch
in place.

Sew the
ends of
the straps
to the
back of
the bag.

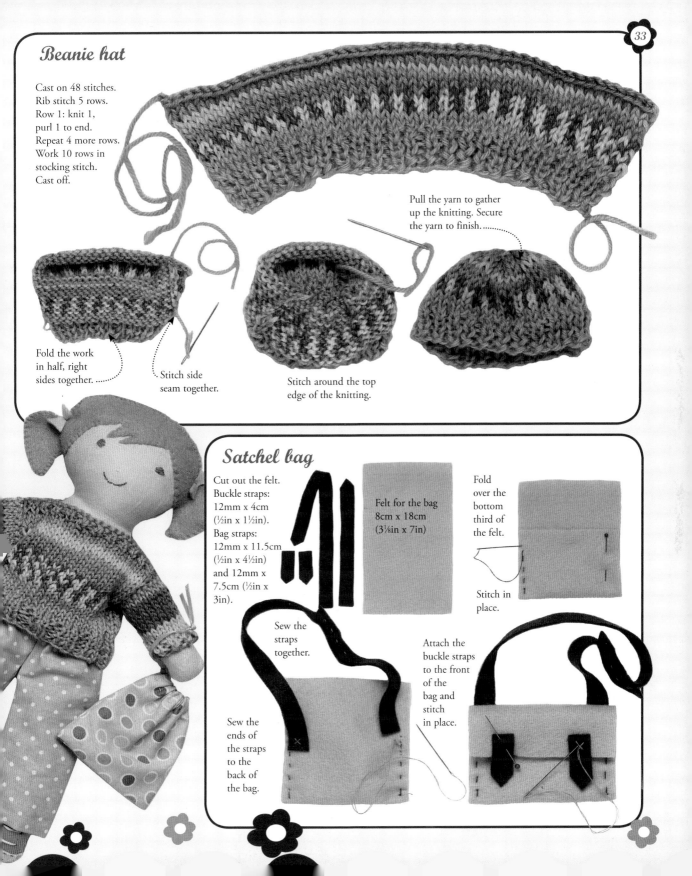

Ballerinas

Lottie goes to a ballet class

The ballerinas' dainty feet are always on tip toe.
Their frilly skirts are made from netting fabric
gathered up to create the perfect tutu effect.

Find the template
for the Lottie doll on pages 13–19

Ballerina tutu and shoes

See the next page to find out how to make the clothes.

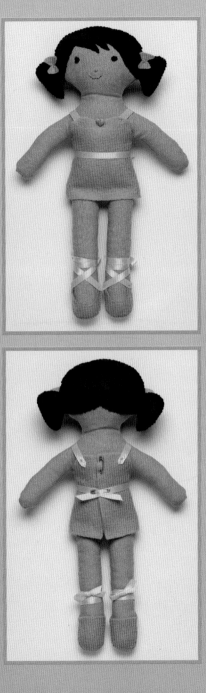

Leotard

A felt bodice with ribbon shoulder straps held at the back with a safety pin and a ribbon waist band.

Tutu skirt

A frothy skirt made with layers of netting fabric gathered up on a ribbon and tied at the back.

Ballet shoes

Dancing shoes made from felt with ribbon ties.

You will need

A BASIC DOLL (pages 13–19) • Sewing kit (pages 112–113)
TUTU SKIRT: 3 pieces of netting fabric 70cm x 19cm (27½in x 7½in),
• Ribbon 40cm (16in) in length
LEOTARD: felt 18cm x 13cm (7in x 5in), 2 pieces of ribbon 10cm (4in)
for shoulder straps, 20cm (8in) for waistband, 2 small safety pins.
SHOES: Scraps of pink felt, 4 lengths of ribbon 20cm (8in).

How to dress a ballerina

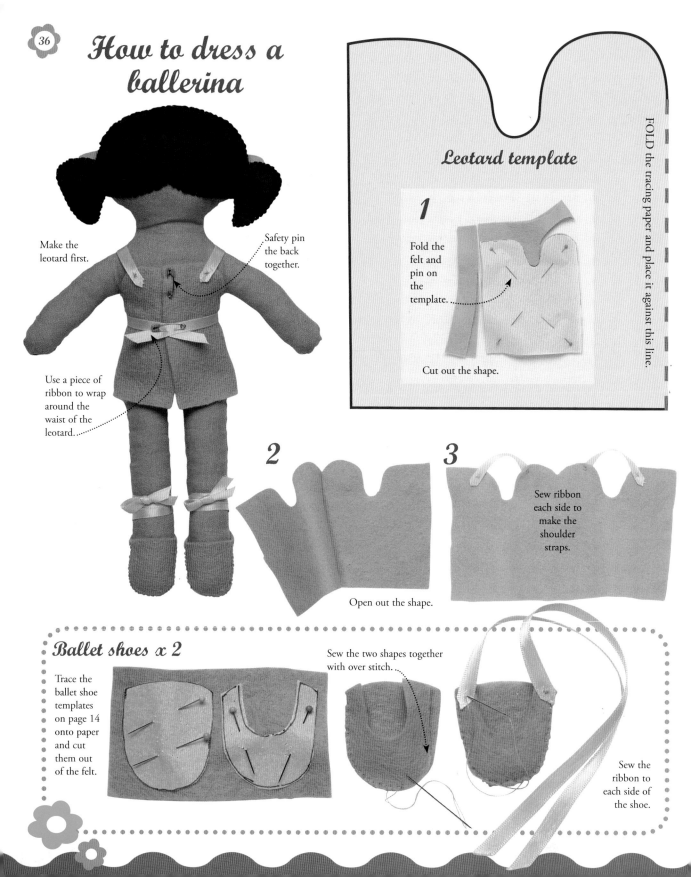

Make the leotard first.

Safety pin the back together.

Use a piece of ribbon to wrap around the waist of the leotard.

Leotard template

FOLD the tracing paper and place it against this line.

1

Fold the felt and pin on the template.

Cut out the shape.

2

Open out the shape.

3

Sew ribbon each side to make the shoulder straps.

Ballet shoes x 2

Trace the ballet shoe templates on page 14 onto paper and cut them out of the felt.

Sew the two shapes together with over stitch.

Sew the ribbon to each side of the shoe.

Tutu skirt

Place the three pieces of netting on top of each other. Fold the whole stack over lengthwise to make one long strip.

Sew along the fold 12mm (½in) from the edge.

Fix a safety pin to one end of the ribbon. Work the pin along the gap in the netting.

Bring the pin through to the other end, gather up the fabric, and tie around the waist.

Fairy wings

A pair of sparkly wings will transform your ballerina doll into a flying fairy. Attach them with pretty ribbons at her shoulders.

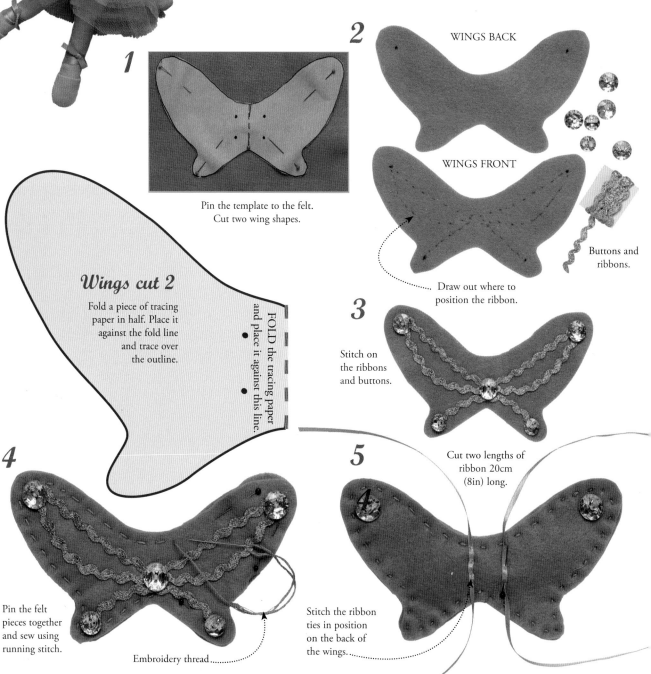

1

Pin the template to the felt. Cut two wing shapes.

2

WINGS BACK

WINGS FRONT

Buttons and ribbons.

Draw out where to position the ribbon.

Wings cut 2

Fold a piece of tracing paper in half. Place it against the fold line and trace over the outline.

FOLD the tracing paper and place it against this line.

3

Stitch on the ribbons and buttons.

4

Pin the felt pieces together and sew using running stitch.

Embroidery thread

5

Cut two lengths of ribbon 20cm (8in) long.

Stitch the ribbon ties in position on the back of the wings.

For wings
You will need

- Sewing kit (pages 112–113)
- Felt fabric
- Buttons and ribbon for decoration
- Ribbon to tie on wings
- Felt pen

Wand

Cut a star from a scrap of felt. Stitch a glittery button to the centre. Fasten the star to a pipe cleaner.

Crown

Cut a strip of felt long enough to fit around the top of her head. Shape the top, bring it round and fasten with a stitch at the back.

Night time

Feeling tired - Lottie and baby Lottie doll are ready for bed.

Baby Lottie doll

Make a baby doll to match Lottie. She has a matching cotton nightie and a felt body. Find the pattern on page 100.

Find the template for the Lottie doll on pages 13–19

Pyjamas and slippers

See the next page to find out how to make clothes.

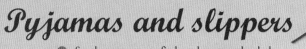

Pyjamas

Make a simple pyjama top gathered at the neck with ribbon.

Pretty bag

Baby Lottie doll

See page 100 to make doll.

The bottoms are baggy trousers made in soft cotton fabric.

Slippers

No nightwear would be complete without extra comfy slippers.

You will need

A BASIC DOLL (pages 13–19) • Sewing kit (pages 112–113)
PYJAMAS: Cotton fabric for pyjama top 25cm x 15cm (10in x 6in)
and bottoms 28cm x 28cm (11in x 11in). Elastic 40cm (7in) • Ribbon 30cm (12in)
SLIPPERS: Scraps of pink, blue, and grey felt.

How to make night clothes

Pyjama bottoms

2 Using backstitch, sew the inside leg seams together up to the dot.

3 Bring the legs together and match up the dots on each leg.

This dot shows where to end your stitching when you sew up the leg seams. Mark it on your fabric..

Sew up to the marked dot.

Stitch the back seam together from the dot marker up to the waist. Repeat this for the front seam.

FOLD LINE for FABRIC

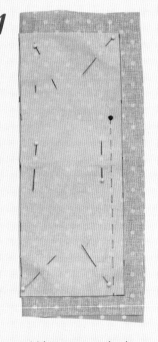

1

Make a paper template by tracing over the lines shown here. Pin the paper to the fabric folded right sides together and cut out.

Pyjama bottoms template cut 2

Slippers x 2

Trace the slipper patterns on page 14 onto paper and cut them out of the felt.

Lottie's doll

See page 100 to follow steps for the tiny doll.

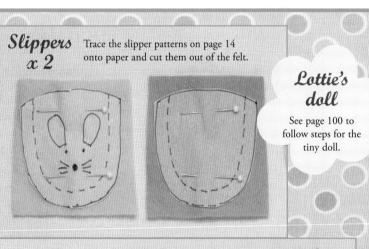

Sew the features onto the front of the slippers.

Sew the two pieces together using running stitch.

Make two slippers.

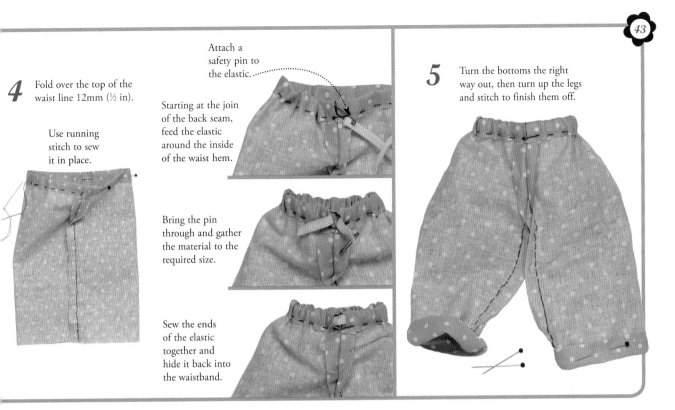

4 Fold over the top of the waist line 12mm (½ in).

Use running stitch to sew it in place.

Attach a safety pin to the elastic.

Starting at the join of the back seam, feed the elastic around the inside of the waist hem.

Bring the pin through and gather the material to the required size.

Sew the ends of the elastic together and hide it back into the waistband.

5 Turn the bottoms the right way out, then turn up the legs and stitch to finish them off.

Nightie Cut a piece of fabric 25cm x 10cm (10in x 4in).

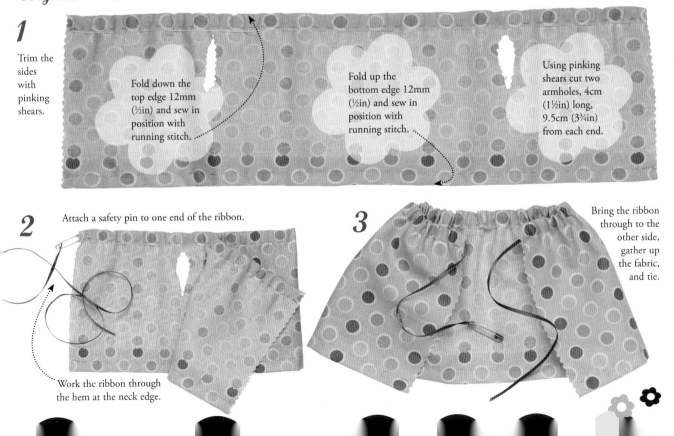

1 Trim the sides with pinking shears.

Fold down the top edge 12mm (½in) and sew in position with running stitch.

Fold up the bottom edge 12mm (½in) and sew in position with running stitch.

Using pinking shears cut two armholes, 4cm (1½in) long, 9.5cm (3¾in) from each end.

2 Attach a safety pin to one end of the ribbon.

Work the ribbon through the hem at the neck edge.

3 Bring the ribbon through to the other side, gather up the fabric, and tie.

Lottie's mix-and-match wardrobe

I'm wrapped up to go out in the cold!

That hat with this bag or this skirt with that sweater? The possibitities are endless.

Shelly the mermaid

Strands of colourful yarn are perfect for Shelly's hair.

... Chunky yarns give a seaweed effect.

Swishing hair and fishy tails

To make a mermaid, use the Lottie doll template on pages 14 for her upper body, head, and arms. Then follow the pattern shown here for her lower body and tail.

Part *a*

Mark these big dots on the fabric. They indicate where to stop sewing and leave the opening for the mermaid's body.

Template for mermaid's tail

You will need

Materials for a BASIC DOLL (pages 13)
• Sewing kit (pages 112–113)
TAIL • Cotton fabric 40cm x 30cm (16in x 12in)
• Soft-toy filling
HAIR • Balls of different coloured yarn • Felt
• Thick card 50cm x 10cm (20in x 4in)
DECORATION • Ribbon, button, and felt

How to make...

A PAPER TEMPLATE FROM THIS TEMPLATE.
Trace out template 'b' then move it over, align it with the top of template 'a', and continue tracing around the shape to make one outline. See over the page, step 1.

Part *b*

These "V" shapes show where to snip the fabric to help shape the doll.

DOTTED LINE shows where to sew your project.

Find the template

for mermaid body on page 14

How to make Shelly the mermaid

1

Make her tail

Take two pieces of fabric and pin the template in place.

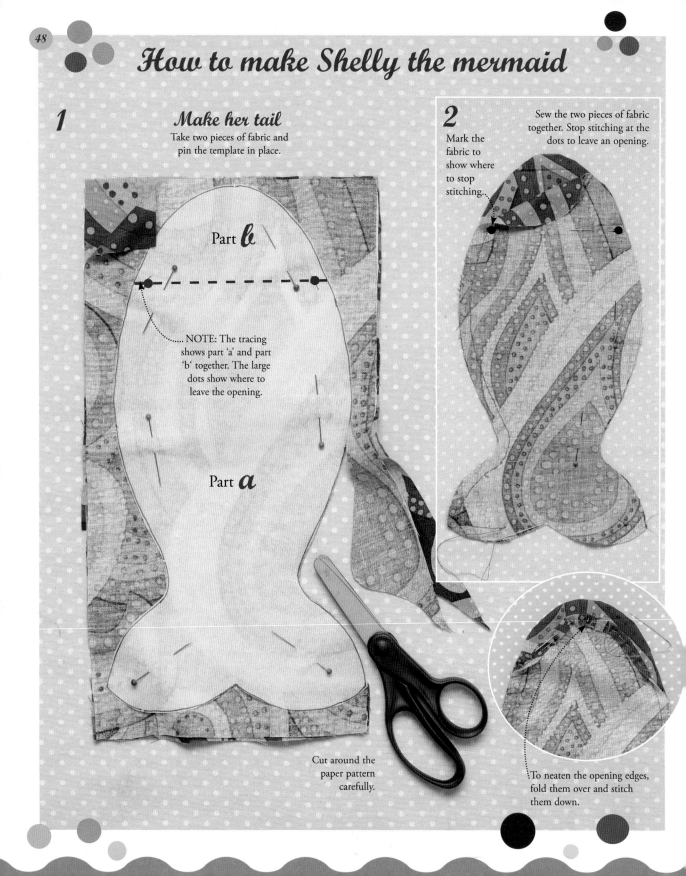

Part **b**

NOTE: The tracing shows part 'a' and part 'b' together. The large dots show where to leave the opening.

Part **a**

Cut around the paper pattern carefully.

2

Mark the fabric to show where to stop stitching...

Sew the two pieces of fabric together. Stop stitching at the dots to leave an opening.

To neaten the opening edges, fold them over and stitch them down.

Make her body and join it to her tail

Make the upper body as shown on pages 14–17.

NOTE: mermaid body is shorter than Lottie doll.

Fill the upper body – don't overfill or it will be difficult to attach to the tail.

Fill the tail – again, don't overfill.

1

Place the upper body inside the tail, and work it into position.

2

Pin the tail to the body, front, back, and sides.

3

Stitch the tail neatly and securely to the body, all the way around.

Shelly's ready for her hair.

1 Start her hair

Pin the hair base patterns to the felt and cut them out.

2

Place the base on to the head and work it into position.

NOTE: Use the template on page 15 for the base shape and follow the steps on page 18 for how to make it.

3

Stitch the base neatly in place all the way around the head.

4 Make her hair

Wrap yarn around a piece of thick card. Wind each colour about four times.

Pull the yarn off the card carefully and tie it up tightly in the middle.

Cut a length of yarn for tying.

Thick card 50cm x 10cm (20in x 4in).

5

Cut another length of yarn and stitch the tresses to her head.

Bring the needle up through the bunch of yarn.

Knot the end of the yarn and bring the needle through.

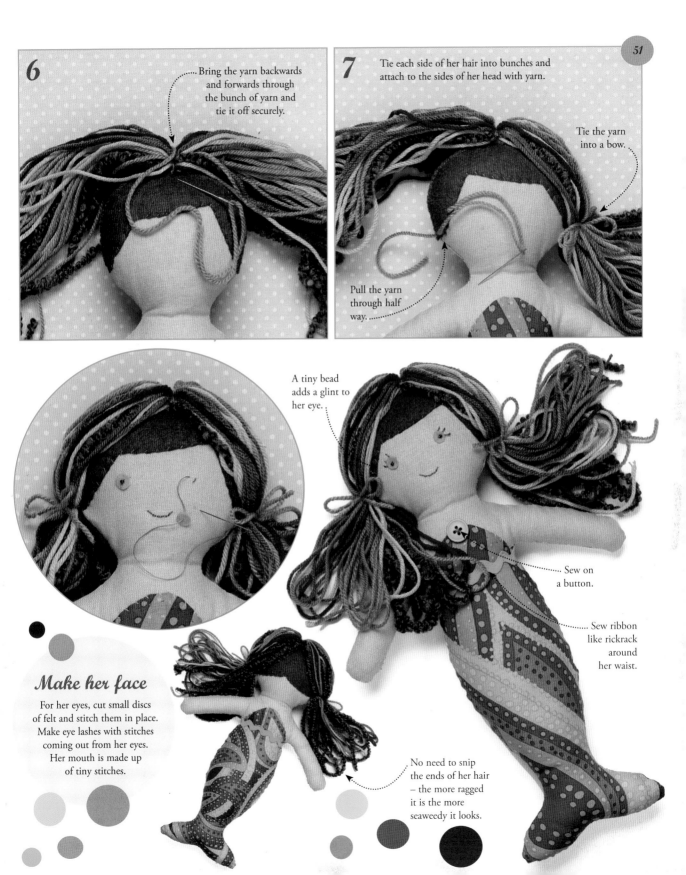

6

Bring the yarn backwards and forwards through the bunch of yarn and tie it off securely.

7 Tie each side of her hair into bunches and attach to the sides of her head with yarn.

Tie the yarn into a bow.

Pull the yarn through half way.

A tiny bead adds a glint to her eye.

Sew on a button.

Sew ribbon like rickrack around her waist.

Make her face

For her eyes, cut small discs of felt and stitch them in place. Make eye lashes with stitches coming out from her eyes. Her mouth is made up of tiny stitches.

No need to snip the ends of her hair – the more ragged it is the more seaweedy it looks.

Cinders

Lucky Cinders!

From her dreary, drab
work clothes she's
magically transformed
into a glamorous princess
ready for the ball.
It's a topsy-turvy world
for this doll.

Cinderella

She shall go to the ball!

How to make Cinders/Cinderella

This topsy-turvy doll has one body with a head either end and four arms. Make up the body and attach the bodice fabric then stitch on the arms.

Arms x 2

Pin the paper template to two layers of fabric.

ARM cut 2

BODY cut 2

ARM cut 2

ARM cut 2

Open out the tracing paper shape and pin it to the fabric

LARGE DOTS
The space between the dots indicates where to leave an opening.

Template for topsy-turvy body

Fold a piece of tracing paper in half. Place the fold against the edge of the template as indicated. Trace around the lines and cut out the paper shape.

These "V" shapes show where to snip the fabric to help shape the doll.

DOTTED LINE
shows where to sew your project.

FOLD TRACING PAPER on this line

You will need

- Sewing Kit (pages 112-113)
TEMPLATE: Tracing paper and pen
DOLL: Lightweight cotton fabric, 2 pieces 18cm x 6.5cm (7in x 3in) • Soft toy filling.
BODICE: Two different lightweight fabrics, each 7cm x 18cm (2¾in x 7½in)
SKIRTS: Two different lightweight fabrics, each 25cm x 54cm (10in x 22in)
- Ribbon 55cm (22in).
CINDERS'S APRON: White cotton fabric 14cm x 15cm (5¾in x 6in)

Make the body

1 Using back stitch sew all the way around the body shape.

Leave an opening for the filling.

2 Turn the body shape right side out and fill evenly.

Fold the edges over and sew up the opening.

Make four arms

1 With right sides together, stitch around two arm pieces leaving the end open.

2 Turn the arm inside out and fill.

NOTE: Only fill the arm half way up.

3 Fold the ends in and pin them together.

4 Sew up the opening neatly.

Dress bodice

1 Fold over the fabric edge 13mm (½in) and stitch it in place.

Cut two pieces of fabric 7cm x 18cm (2¾in x 7in).

2 Place the fabrics together with right sides facing. Pin in place.

Sew the two pieces together using running stitch.

3 Open out the fabric. Fold the edge over and stitch it in down.

Wrap the bodice around the doll and pin it in position.

Bring the other end to meet it and sew it in place.

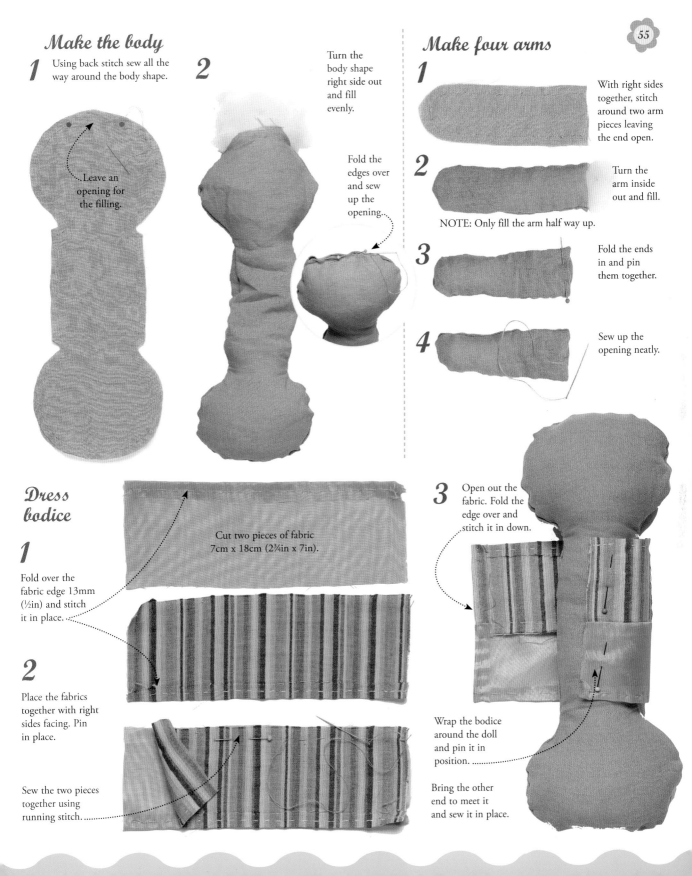

Pin one pair of arms to each half of the bodice.

Decorating the dolls

Prepare the felt hair pieces and attach them as shown on pages 18–19. Decorate the two bodices, add accessories, and stitch on the faces.

Stitch together Cinderella's hair and attach it to her head.

Cut out a felt tiara and rickrack decoration.

Cut two strips of rickrack. Wrap them crosswise around the chest and sew them in place.

Back of doll

Rickrack bracelet

Make sure the arms are in the right position and overstitch the edges to attach them securely.

Cut a strip of rickrack and wrap it around the top of the dress. Stitch in position.

Stitch together Cinders's hair and attach it to her head.

Hair for Cinderella doll

Trace the shapes onto tracing paper and follow the steps on page 18–19 to attach the hair.

You will need

• Sewing Kit (pages 112-113)
HAIR: Felt fabric, 2 pieces 18cm x 18cm (7in x 7in) for each head.
DECORATION: Selection of rickrack, sequins, and beads.

Decorate with beads and sequins.

Hair for Cinders doll

Trace the shapes onto tracing paper and follow the steps on pages 18–19 to attach the hair.

Stitch on eyes and a mouth following the steps on page 19.

How to make a topsy-turvy skirt

1 Cut the skirt material to the required size.

Sew the apron to the centre of Cinders's skirt, at the top of the skirt fabric.

3 Open the fabric out and hem each skirt by turning up the edge 2cm (¾in).

Use running stitch to hem the skirts.

2 Place the second skirt fabric over the first, right sides together.

Stitch the two together with running stitch.

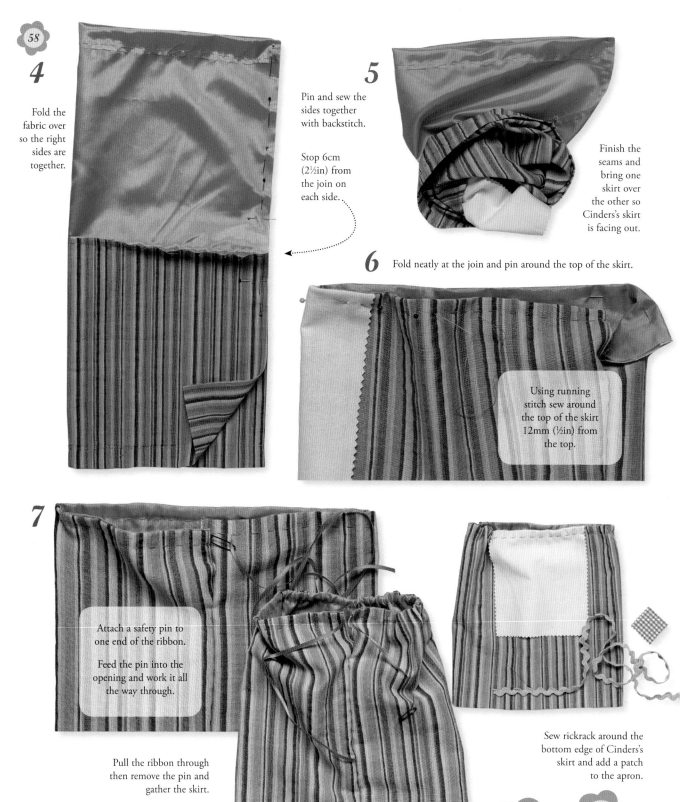

4

Fold the fabric over so the right sides are together.

5

Pin and sew the sides together with backstitch.

Stop 6cm (2½in) from the join on each side.

Finish the seams and bring one skirt over the other so Cinders's skirt is facing out.

6 Fold neatly at the join and pin around the top of the skirt.

Using running stitch sew around the top of the skirt 12mm (½in) from the top.

7

Attach a safety pin to one end of the ribbon.

Feed the pin into the opening and work it all the way through.

Pull the ribbon through then remove the pin and gather the skirt.

Sew rickrack around the bottom edge of Cinders's skirt and add a patch to the apron.

Finishing the doll

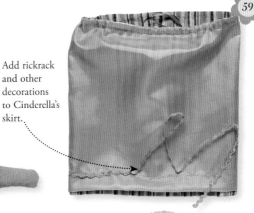

Handy tip

Tie the ribbon tight around
the waist. To prevent the skirt
from slipping up and down,
add a few stitches anchoring
the top of the skirt to
the waistline.

Sit the skirt on
the waistline
and arrange
the gathers.

Place the doll inside the
skirt, gather it up and tie
the ribbon into a bow.

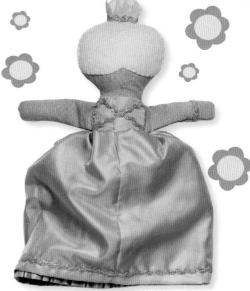

Wakey, wakey...

Sleepy and awake - here's a simple alternative for a topsy-turvy doll.

Position the skirt at the waistline then sew to the bodice fabric.

To make your doll

Follow the steps for Cinders/Cinderella on the previous pages. Choose different patterned fabric for her nightie and day dress. Her hair is made using the template on page 15 – for the face see page 19.

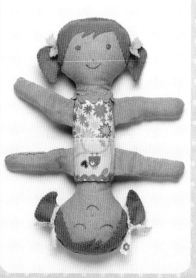

...rise and shine

Pillow and nightie

Make a pillow from leftover nightie fabric.

Day dress

2

Woolly

dolls

Go knit yourself

Make a doll that looks like you Simply follow this knitting pattern to create your own doll. The coloured stripes will make up the parts of the body.

"Hi, I'm Jane Bull"

Yarn for skin

Yarn for top

Yarn for shorts

Yarn for shoes

Hey! You will need

- Sewing kit (pages 112–113)
- Knitting needles 4mm (No 6) • Stitch holder
- Balls of DK knitting yarn:

1 ball for skin colour • 1 ball for top

1 ball for shorts • 1 ball for shoes

1 ball for hair • Tapestry needle

- Soft-toy filling

You choose how you want your doll to look. Simply change the colours of the stripes you knit.

Don't change colour here – knit an all-in-one.

Ring the changes with bands of colour.

Scarlet

Cherry

Sarah

How to make a knitted doll

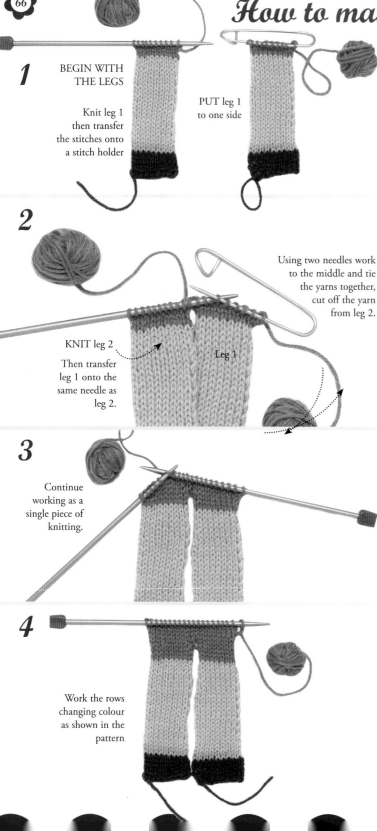

1 BEGIN WITH THE LEGS

Knit leg 1 then transfer the stitches onto a stitch holder

PUT leg 1 to one side

2 Using two needles work to the middle and tie the yarns together, cut off the yarn from leg 2.

KNIT leg 2

Then transfer leg 1 onto the same needle as leg 2.

Leg 1

3 Continue working as a single piece of knitting.

4 Work the rows changing colour as shown in the pattern

To knit the body

Use stocking stitch (see page 121).

Begin with the legs - see steps 1-4

LEG 1 Cast on 14 stitches in shoe colour, work 6 rows starting with knit stitch. change to sock colour, work 2 rows. change to skin colour, work 21 rows. Change to shorts colour, work 4 rows. Transfer the stitches from the needle onto a stich holder and set aside.

LEG 2 Repeat working as for leg 1 but keep the work on the needle.

BODY and HEAD Transfer the stitches from the stitch holder onto the needle – holding leg 2. Work 8 rows. Change to top colour and work 21 rows. Change to skin colour and work 21 rows. Cast off.

To knit the arms

Use stocking stitch.

Cast on 10 stitches in the skin colour yarn and work 6 rows. Change to wrist colour and work 2 rows. Change to top colour and work 20 rows. Cast off.

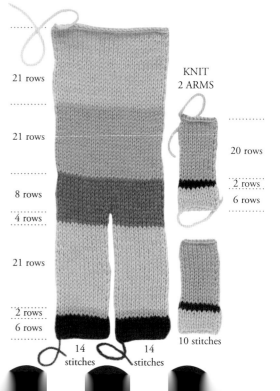

21 rows

21 rows

8 rows

4 rows

21 rows

2 rows

6 rows

14 stitches   14 stitches

KNIT 2 ARMS

20 rows

2 rows

6 rows

10 stitches

Make up the body

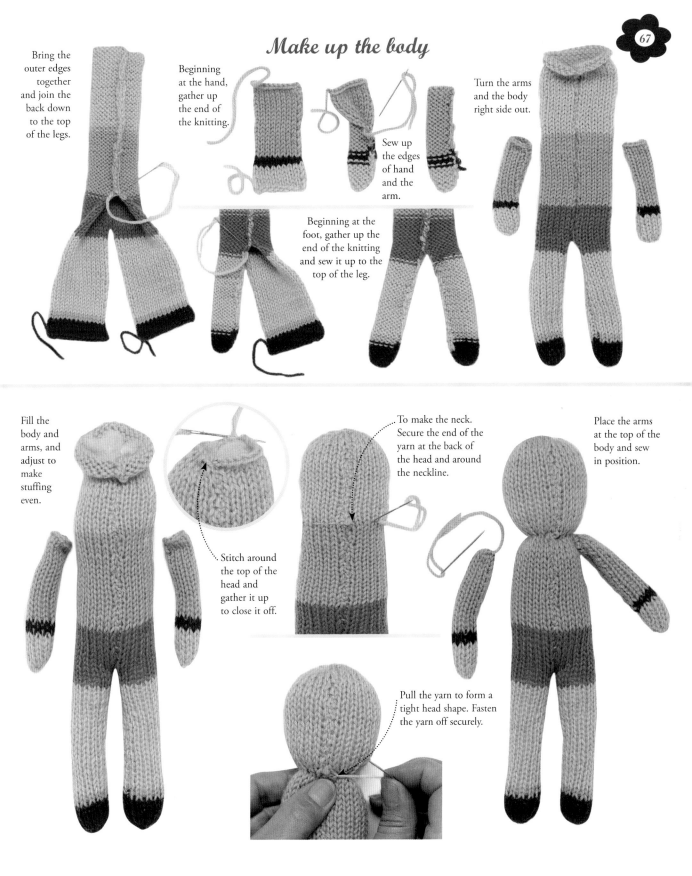

Bring the outer edges together and join the back down to the top of the legs.

Beginning at the hand, gather up the end of the knitting.

Sew up the edges of hand and the arm.

Turn the arms and the body right side out.

Beginning at the foot, gather up the end of the knitting and sew it up to the top of the leg.

Fill the body and arms, and adjust to make stuffing even.

Stitch around the top of the head and gather it up to close it off.

To make the neck. Secure the end of the yarn at the back of the head and around the neckline.

Place the arms at the top of the body and sew in position.

Pull the yarn to form a tight head shape. Fasten the yarn off securely.

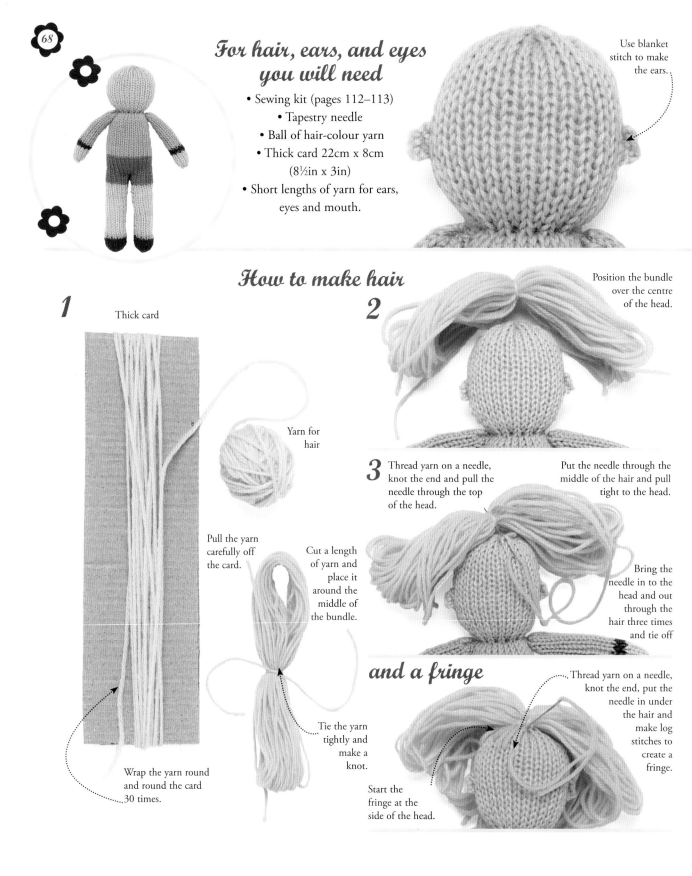

For hair, ears, and eyes you will need

- Sewing kit (pages 112–113)
- Tapestry needle
- Ball of hair-colour yarn
- Thick card 22cm x 8cm (8½in x 3in)
- Short lengths of yarn for ears, eyes and mouth.

Use blanket stitch to make the ears.

How to make hair

1

Thick card

Yarn for hair

Pull the yarn carefully off the card.

Wrap the yarn round and round the card 30 times.

Cut a length of yarn and place it around the middle of the bundle.

Tie the yarn tightly and make a knot.

2

Position the bundle over the centre of the head.

3

Thread yarn on a needle, knot the end and pull the needle through the top of the head.

Put the needle through the middle of the hair and pull tight to the head.

Bring the needle in to the head and out through the hair three times and tie off

and a fringe

Thread yarn on a needle, knot the end, put the needle in under the hair and make log stitches to create a fringe.

Start the fringe at the side of the head.

How to make ears

1 Thread a length of yarn on the needle and knot the end. Put the yarn into the side of the head and make a stitch.

2 Make four stitches from left to right.

3 Working into the four stitches already made, work back from right to left.

To finish, make a couple of stitches into the head and cut off the thread.

How to make a face

Decide what kind of face your doll will have. Use woollen yarn to make the features.

1 Bring the yarn through the back of the head

Sew the mouth shape using back stitch

2 Bring the yarn back to the side of the head and snip off the yarn and the knot.

Repeat step 1 and 2 for the eyes.

TIP FOR SEWING FEATURES
To hide the ends of the thread, firstly knot the end of the yarn and bring it through the side of the head and out to the front, where you want to position the mouth. Sew the mouth shape, then bring the yarn back through to the side of the head. Snip off the yarn and the knot.

Bags and beads

To knit a bag

Use stocking stitch (page 121).
Cast on 20 stitches.
Work 32 rows in main colour.
Cast off.

1 Fold the rectangle in half with the correct sides facing in.

Sew down the edges each side.

2 Sew the handles to each side of the bag.

FOR THE HANDLES – turn to page 123. Make 34 chain stitches. Leave the strands either end to sew to the bag.

The handles are made of a foundation chain using a crochet hook. See page 123 to find out.

You can make larger bags by increasing the number of stitches and rows you use.

To knit a skirt

Use stocking stitch (page 121).
Cast on 60 stitches.
Work 22 rows in main colour, beginning with a knit row.
Row 23: knit 2 together, knit 1.
Repeat to end. (40 stitches remain).
Row 24: purl to end.
Row 25: knit 2, knit 2 together.
Repeat to end. (30 stitches remain).
Row 26: purl to end.
Row 27 and 28: knit and purl row in contrasting colour.
Note: don't cut off the main colour, leave it until it's needed again.
Row 29: knit in main colour to end.
Cast off.

Your knitting should flare out as shown here.

Leave the loose ends and use them for stitching the skirt together.

Fold the knitting in half (with the correct sides facing in) and stitch the sides together.

The finished skirt is ready to go.

To make a necklace

With a needle and thread tie a knot around one of the beads.

Thread the beads onto the thread.

Threading complete

Pass the needle back through the first bead a few times and make a knot.

Attach to the doll by stitching in and out of the doll and the necklace. Secure the thread and cut it off.

Hair styles

Make a tidy style by tying the hair into bunches. Sew a length of yarn each side of the head and tie it around the hair in a bow. She could try wearing her hair up in a bun too.

Add beads for earrings.

Skirts and bags

Experiment with the design of the skirt
to suit your doll. Here's a fancy one that's
got the pattern knitted into it. Try this by
changing the colour of the yarn as you knit
making stitches in a different colour
to create a patterned effect.

Make mini-knitting

Complete the look for your dolls with tiny knitting needles and yarn. Take two wooden cocktail sticks, glue a bead to the end of each one. Then, to make the knitting, just cast on in the usual way and get started!

Pirate Pete

For his ears follow the steps on pages 68–69.

Use black yarn to stitch an eye patch and black felt for his moustache.

His earrings are loops of gold thread stitched to his ears.

To make a rolled-up trouser effect, knit stitch the first row of the trouser then knit, purl, and knit the next three rows. This will give a raised effect to the front of the work. Then continue to work in stocking stitch.

.... For his gold belt, use gold thread and stitch a buckle shape.

How to make pirates and heroes

These dolls use the same method as those on pages 64–68. Make up your doll following the steps. Match the colours to the dolls shown here or choose your own colourways.

You will need

- Colourful knitting yarn
- Size 4 (No 6) knitting needles
- Tapestry needle
- Soft-toy filling
- Sewing kit (pages 112-113)

To knit the body

Use stocking stitch (page 121). Begin with the legs.
LEG 1 • Cast on 14 stitches in black. BOOTS – work 12 rows beginning with knit stitch. TROUSERS – work 22 rows in brown, transfer stitches to stitch holder. LEG 2 • Repeat as for leg 1. BODY • Place stitches onto one needle and continue trousers. Work 9 rows. BELT – work 3 rows in black. SHIRT – work 14 rows in stripes, two rows per stripe, alternating with white and blue. HEAD • work 13 rows in flesh colour. HAT – work 8 rows in red. Cast off.

To knit the arms

Use stocking stitch (page 121). Cast on 10 stitches
HANDS • work 6 rows in flesh colour. SHIRT SLEEVES • work 20 rows in stripes of two rows for each colour, white and blue. Cast off.

Superhero

To knit the body

Use stocking stitch (page 121).
Begin with the legs.
LEG 1 • Cast on 14 stitches in purple. BOOTS – work 12 rows beginning with knit stitch. Work 2 rows in blue stripe. TROUSERS – work 22 rows, then transfer stitches to stitch holder.
LEG 2 • Repeat as for leg 1.
BODY • Place stitches onto one needle and change to blue for shorts, work 9 rows. BELT – work 3 rows in purple. SHIRT – work 15 rows in yellow. HEAD • FACE - work 8 rows in flesh colour. MASK - work 4 rows in purple, work 1 row in blue. HAT - work 8 rows in yellow. Cast off.

To knit the arms

Use stocking stitch (page 121).
Cast on 10 stitches in flesh colour.
HANDS • work 6 rows.
SHIRT SLEEVES • Work one stripe in blue, then work 19 rows in yellow. Cast off.

To knit a cape

Use stocking stitch (page 121).
Cast on 60 stitches in blue.
Work 22 rows in main colour, beginning with a knit row.
Row 23: knit 2 together, knit 1.
Repeat to end. (40 stitches remain)
Row 24: purl to end.
Row 25: knit 2, knit 2 together.
Repeat to end. (30 stitches remain)
Row 26: purl to end.
Work 3 more rows.
Cast off.

To attach the cape, stitch it to the back of the head at the neckline.

Make three stitches for his Superhero "S" symbol.

Stitch a cross stitch for his buckle.

The glovables

Turn unwanted gloves into loveable characters. Here, Daisy Doll shows off her petal hair and skirt right down to her boots.

Little Baby

Mister Orange

Daisy Doll

You will need

- A selection of odd gloves Soft-toy filling
- Sewing kit (pages 112–113)
- Yarn for features
- Buttons for eyes

TOP: Finger tips make petals and ears.

1 Turn the gloves inside out. Stitch up the the finger and thumb holes to close them up, as shown.

Cut off unwanted finger and thumb to use for the arms.

2 Turn the gloves right side out.

Fill the head to make a firm ball shape.

Fill the body and arms.

3

Stitch around the base of the head, gather it up tight and secure in place.

Cut off the excess bit of cuff and keep for Daisy's skirt.

TOP TIP: If the gloves are too long – cut some off the cuff to make a better fit.

4 Attach the head to the body. Tuck the head into the top of the other glove and pin in position.

Sew up the ends of the arms.

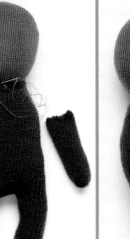

5

Sew the arms in position on the sides of the body.

Arrange fingertips around the head.

Stitch the petals in position from the back.

6

Use yarn for the eyebrows, nose, and mouth.

Use buttons for the eyes.

7

Daisy's skirt and boots

Use the cuff from the "head" glove to make a waistband.

Spare fingers from other gloves make the skirt.

To make the skirt, choose nine fingers from your collection of gloves, and stitch them neatly to the underside of the waistband.

For Daisy's boots, use two leftover fingers.

Other glovables

Little Baby is simply made from two matching gloves using the same method as for Daisy Doll. Just add ears, a button at the belly, and a few strands of yarn for the hair. Give Orange Man a rollneck sweater by retaining the cuff on the glove body. Stitch his hair using black yarn and make a woolly hat from the cuff off another glove.

For his rollneck top, leave the cuff of the body glove attached.

Stitch on a belly button.

Tiny folk

You will need
- Sewing kit (pages 112–113)
- Colourful knitting yarn
- Size 4 (No 6) knitting needles
- Tapestry needle
- Soft-toy filling

Knitted little people are a bit fiddly, but fun to make.
What better way to use up your scraps of yarn?

1

BODY

Work in stocking stitch (page 121). Cast on 12 stitches, work a total of 13 rows for the body and 8 rows for the head. Cast off.

Gather up the top

2

Fold the knitting in half right sides together and join the edges.

Turn the knitting right side out and fill it up.

3

Wrap yarn around the neck to make a head shape.

ARMS and LEGS

Work in stocking stitch.
For the arms: cast on 4 stitches, work 9 rows, and cast off.
For the legs: cast on 4 stitches, work 12 rows, and cast off.

Use the ends of the yarn to attach the limbs to the body.

4

Finished and ready to decorate.

Sew the loose end back into the limb to tidy it away.

Place each limb in position against the body and stitch it in place.

For long hair, gather up strands of yarn and fasten it to the centre of the head.

For hair, use yarn and sew short and long stitches from the centre of the head outwards.

The dolls can have rounded bodies too. Simply gather up like the head end.

Use yarn to make the eyes and mouth.

Make a brooch

To turn one of your tiny dolls into a brooch, just stitch a safety pin to the back and fasten it on!

Tiny variations

Be creative – make your folk bigger by casting on more stitches and adding more rows. Do the same for longer or shorter limbs.

Sew in and out around the waist to make a belt.

The good the bad and the cuddly

This clutch of characters is easy to make. Simply knit some stripy square shapes, sew them up, and add filling until they're soft and cuddly. Even the baddies are softies!

You will need

- Sewing kit (pages 112–113)
- Knitting needles 4mm (No 6)
- Balls of DK knitting yarn:
  - Tapestry needle
  - Soft-toy filling

How to knit a hero

Knit some stripes

Use stocking stitch
(page 121).
Begin with the legs.
STRIPE 1: Cast on 28
stitches in red, work 11
rows starting with knit stitch.
STRIPE 2: Change to shorts
black, work 7 rows.
STRIPE 3: Change to yellow,
work 1 row.
STRIPE 4: Change to red,
work 10 rows.
STRIPE 5: Change to flesh
colour, work 7 rows.
STRIPE 6: Change to
black, work 4 rows.
STRIPE 7: Change to red,
work 7 rows.
Cast off.

Knitted
stripes

7

6

5

4

3

2

1

Begin with the legs, cast on 28 stitches

1

Fold the knitting in half
and stitch the edges
right sides together.

2

Bring the
join to the
centre and
stitch the
top end
together.

NOTE: TO MAKE ROUND
SHAPED HEADS
Stitch around the top edge of the
knitting, pull on the thread to gather it
up, secure the thread and cut off.

3

Turn right side
out, fill the shape
and stitch up the
opening at the
base.

4

Pull the end of the
yarn tight and sew
some extra stitches
to keep it in place.

Sew a running
stitch around the
base of the face
stripe. Gather up
to make a
rounded head
shape.

Secure
the yarn
tightly.

Shape arms and legs

To make the arm and leg shapes, stitch through the body as indicated by the dotted lines.

Hold the doll's body where the legs will be.

Bring the needle from front to back.

Stitch down to the feet area and fasten off.

Repeat for the arms. Position as indicated by the dotted lines.

Adding features

Once the doll is complete, add some personal touches. See steps on page 69 for how to stitch the eyes, mouth and other features.

Shape the hat

Shape the peaks and pin them in position.

Pinch the corner of the head and stitch across to form a peak.

Make a face

Use yarn to make the eyes and mouth.

Action Boy

Make a symbol with three stitches.

Zombie alien thing

► KNIT
7 STRIPES
1: 4 rows
2: 1 row
3: 10 rows
4: 1 row
5: 1 row
6: 21 rows
7: 4 rows

Mystery hero

Use single stitches for each eye and the mouth.

Use two stitches for each eye.

.To make her braids, thread three strands of yarn at the side of the head and plait.

◄ KNIT
6 STRIPES
1: 4 rows
2: 12 rows
3: 2 rows
4: 11 rows
5: 6 rows
6: 11 rows

► KNIT
5 STRIPES
1: 4 rows
2: 12 rows
3: 13 rows
4: 10 rows
5: 10 rows

Colourful characters

These are created by changing the colour and depth of the stripes (see page 83). Starting with the feet (stripe 1), cast on 28 stitches and follow the number of stripes and rows for each one.

Action Girl

Jolly Roger

Make a patch using black yarn.

► KNIT
11 STRIPES
1: 4 rows
2: 10 rows
3: 2 rows
4: 2 rows
5: 2 rows
6: 2 rows
7: 2 rows
8: 2 rows
9: 1 row
10: 13 rows
11: 5 rows

Ninja kid

► KNIT
6 STRIPES
1: 15 rows
2: 2 rows
3: 18 rows
4: 3 rows
5: 2 rows
6: 7 rows

Add Ninja features by attaching yarn to the head and to the waist.

Cool dude

► KNIT
9 STRIPES
1: 4 rows
2: 12 rows
3: 7 rows
4: 2 rows
5: 11 rows
6: 8 rows
7: 2 rows
8: 2 rows
9: 3 rows

You will need

- Piece of card 20cm x 8cm (8in x 3in)
- Balls of colourful yarn
- Scissors

Multi-coloured dolls

This project is a great way to use up all your scraps of yarn. Start wrapping the yarn around the card as shown; you can add a new colour when it runs out.

Yarn dolls

Swishing dancers - here's a simple project that will transform your colourful leftover yarns into fun swaying dolls.

1 Wrap the yarn around the card about 40 times.

2 Cut a short piece of yarn and tie the bundle together tightly at the top. Remove card.

3 Make a head shape. Tie a length of yarn about 3.5cm (1½in) from the top.

4 Cut through all the loops at the bottom.

5 Separate the bundle into the body and two arms. Tie yarn around the body to make the waist.

Arm

Arm

Body

6 Hang up your yarn doll with the yarn used to tie up the bundle.

Tie yarn around the arms to make the wrists.

Trim the ends of the yarn for a neat finish.

Colourways

Play with the colours of your dolls. Try using contrasting colours for the yarn tied around the waist, head, and arms. The more clashing the better.

3

Dolly
mixtures

Lavender girls

A fresh take on lavender bags – dolls dresses filled with aromatic herbs can hang with your clothes to make them smell sweet.

1

Prepare all the doll pieces.

Using tracing paper, trace over the shapes on the page opposite.

Cut out the paper pieces, pin to the fabric and cut out.

Use pinking shears to prevent the edge fraying.

You will need
Sewing kit (pages 112-113)
BODY PARTS • Scraps of felt fabric
DRESS • Cotton fabric 13cm x 13cm (5in x 5in)
• 2 tablespons of dried lavender • Paper for funnel
• Ribbon 23cm (9in) and a button • Pinking shears

2

Embroidery thread

Leave the top open.

Dried lavender

Make a funnel out of paper and place it in the opening. Pour the lavender into the dress.

Sew the two dress pieces together using running stitch, leaving an opening at the top.

Stitch two arm pieces together.

Attach the arms to the back of the dress.

Bring the hands to the front.

Fold both leg pieces in half and stitch together.

Attach the legs to the back of the dress.

3

Place the top of the dress in between the head pieces and pin in place.

Sew all the layers together.

Place the edge of each leg in the centre of a shoe shape.

Fold the shoe over and stitch the two sides together.

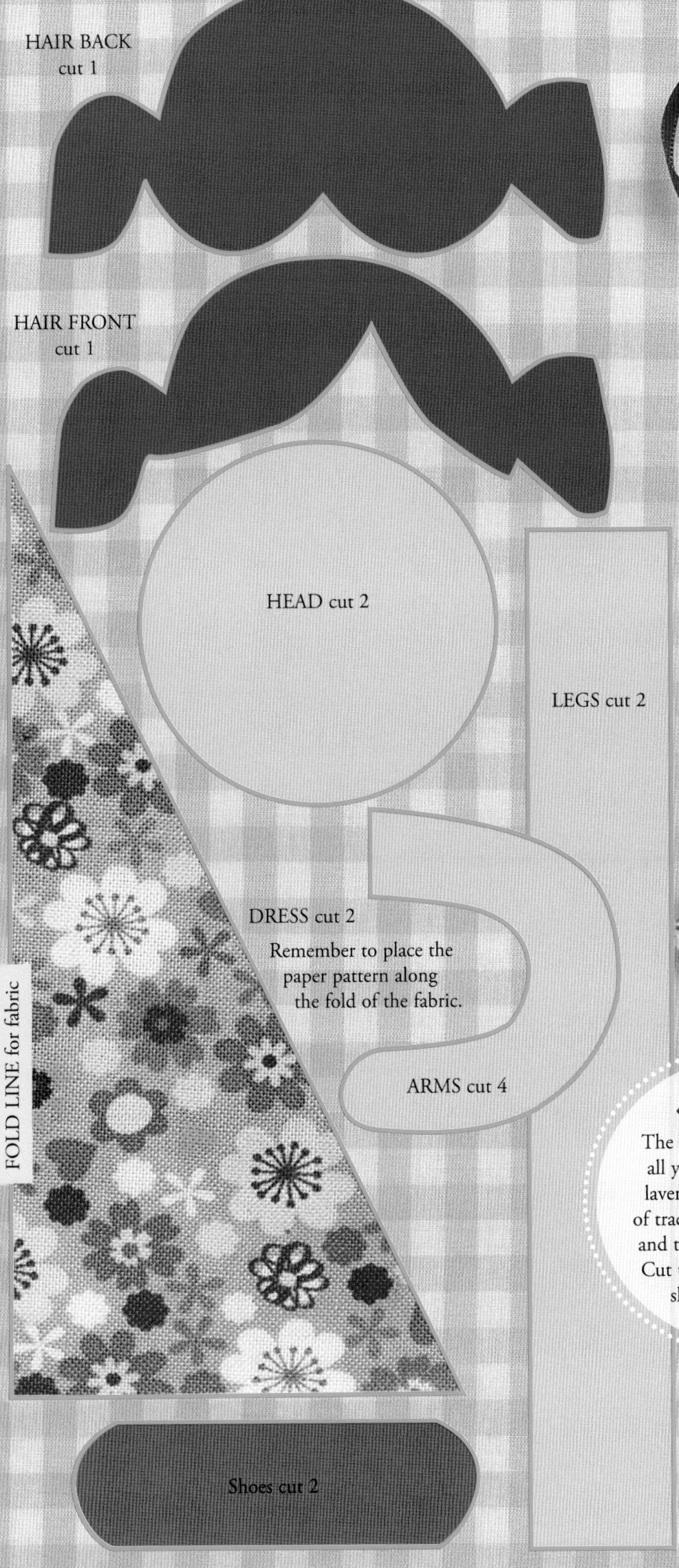

HAIR BACK
cut 1

HAIR FRONT
cut 1

HEAD cut 2

LEGS cut 2

DRESS cut 2
Remember to place the
paper pattern along
the fold of the fabric.

ARMS cut 4

FOLD LINE for fabric

Shoes cut 2

Ribbon

Place the ends of
the ribbon at the back
of the head and stitch
them in place with the
button on the front.

Template

The shapes on this page are
all you need to make your
lavender doll. Place a piece
of tracing paper over the page
and trace around the shapes.
Cut them out and place the
shapes on the fabric.

More lavender ladies to hang around

Rickrack ribbon

How to make
Make these dolls in the same way as the the one shown on pages 90–91. Follow the steps and make variations to suit your own doll.

VEIL
Cut a strip of netting, gather it up along the edge and stitch it all the way round the head.

FANCY RIBBON
Stitch the ribbon to the base of the dress, and around the neck and use it to finish off the headdress.

White cotton dress

Lavender bride

BOUQUET
To make a bouquet, cut out small discs of felt with pinking shears. Sew a felt flower shape onto the discs. Sew the bouquet onto the dress.

FUNKY LEGS
Pick up the colours in the fabric to give her coordinating legs, shoes, and hair.

Lavender girl

Place your doll on a coat hanger and hang her in your wardrobe.

Lavender fairy

Use a band of felt for the crown.

Use pinking shears to create fancy edges.

Fairy wings

Fold a piece of felt 6cm x 8cm 2½in x 3¼in) in half. Use pinking shears to cut an oval shape. Open out the shape, place it in the centre of the fairy's back and neatly stitch it to the dress down the middle of the wings.

Pull the thread to gather up the fabric. This will give her legs shape.

Doodle dolls

Bring your doodles to life by tracing the drawings onto fabric to create fun-shaped cushions.

1 Draw a few doodles on a piece of paper.

2 Cut a piece of fabric larger than each one of your doodles. Leave at least 5cm (2in) space around the edges of your drawing.

Place the fabric over your doodle.

Using the permanent pen, trace over the drawing. Or you can draw a doodle right onto the fabric.

You will need
- Sewing kit (pages 112–113)
- Paper and pens for doodling
- White cotton fabric
- Colourful cotton fabric
- Permanent pens for drawing on fabric • Pencil
- Soft-toy filling

3 Turn the fabric over so the drawing is showing reverse side up. .....

Draw a pencil line 2cm (¾in) away from the image.

4 Take a piece of colouful fabric, right side up and place the drawing on top.

Pin the pieces of fabric together.

Use running stitch to sew along the pencil outline.

.........Leave an opening at the base.

Picture size

If your doodles aren't the size you want, try reducing or enlarging them on a photocopier. Use the enlarged image to trace over.

TIP:
Leaving the extra space around your drawing allows it to sit on top of the cushion and not disappear over the sides.

1 Cut away the extra fabric, 15mm (½in) from the stitch line.

2 Turn the drawing right side out.

Fill up the doll so it's nicely padded.

3 Fold in the edges of the fabric and sew up the opening neatly.

Small doodle dolls would make good pin or needle holders.

Bright fabric backing

To add some colour to your dolls, try mixing and matching the backing fabric. Any lightweight cotton is suitable.

Colourful characters

Complete your doodle dolls by colouring them in. Use any permanent or fabric pens and colour in the drawings, just like you would on paper.

I'm a princess, I look even more beautiful coloured in.

Little Lotties

Every Lottie needs a Little Lottie and maybe even a littler Lottie too.
Make a drawstring bag to keep them all in.

You will need
- Sewing kit (page 112–113)
- Felt in assorted colours
- Soft-toy filling
- Cotton fabric for dresses and bags

How to make Little Lotties

Little Lottie templates

Place tracing paper over the shapes. Trace over the lines and cut out.

Baby Lottie templates

1

Pin the template pieces to the felt.

CUT 2

CUT 2

Cut out the shapes you want.

2

Leave an opening at the top of the doll.

Pin the body shapes together.

3

Fill the doll and sew up the opening.

Neatly stitch the edges together using overstitch.

4

Sew the two hair pieces together.

Fit the hair on to the head and stitch in place.

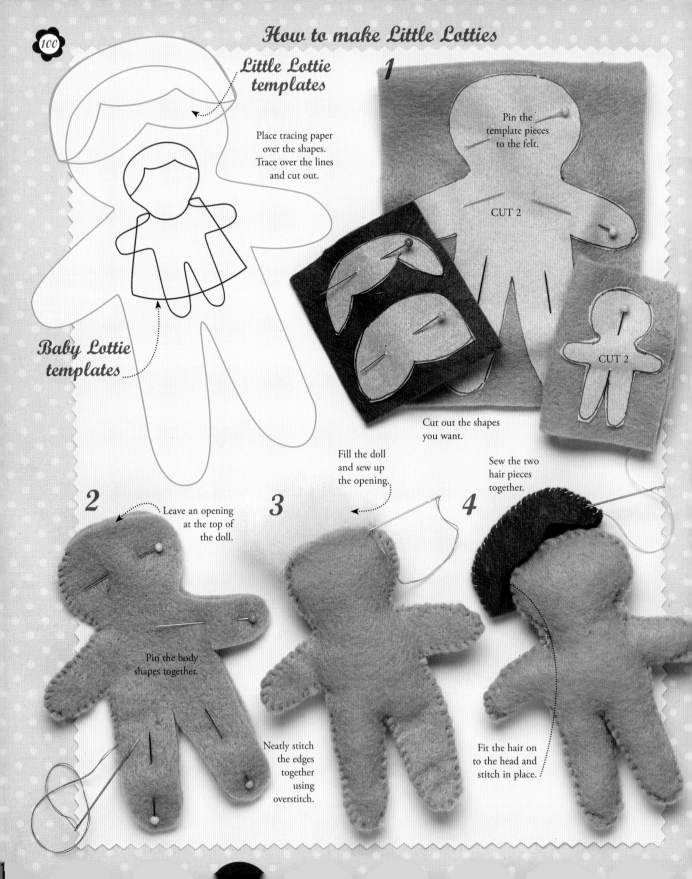

How to make Baby Lotties

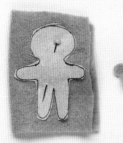

Cut out two doll shapes.

Cut out the felt hair and sew together.

FRONT   BACK

Sew on the hair and face to the front piece.

Place the front and back pieces together.

Stitch them using small running stitches.

Cut out two dress shapes and two bows.

BOWS

DRESS

Dolly bags

Each doll can have its very own bag with a drawstring top. Find out how to make them on page 102.

On the doll, stitch the dress pieces together at the shoulders and under the arms.

Add little felt shapes to the front of the dress for decoration.

Decorate the edge and top of the dress with fancy stitches.

Finishing your Little Lottie

Make a face and add bows

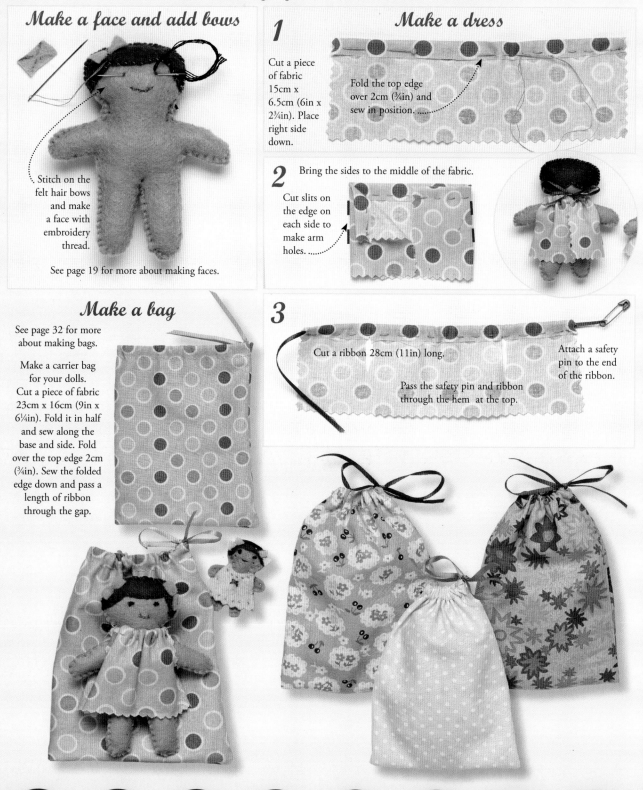

Stitch on the felt hair bows and make a face with embroidery thread.

See page 19 for more about making faces.

Make a dress

1 Cut a piece of fabric 15cm x 6.5cm (6in x 2¾in). Place right side down.

Fold the top edge over 2cm (¾in) and sew in position.

2 Bring the sides to the middle of the fabric.

Cut slits on the edge on each side to make arm holes.

3 Cut a ribbon 28cm (11in) long.

Pass the safety pin and ribbon through the hem at the top.

Attach a safety pin to the end of the ribbon.

Make a bag

See page 32 for more about making bags.

Make a carrier bag for your dolls. Cut a piece of fabric 23cm x 16cm (9in x 6¼in). Fold it in half and sew along the base and side. Fold over the top edge 2cm (¾in). Sew the folded edge down and pass a length of ribbon through the gap.

Mix and match dolls

Match the baby to the doll. The variations for these little dolls are endless, so experiment with colours and fabrics.

Cut out tiny bows and felt shapes to decorate the dolls.

Finish the edges with pinking shears.

Pillow dolls

Plump up your pillows! Draw square and rectangle shapes and create characters inside the lines.

You will need
- Sewing kit (pages 112–113)
- White cotton fabric
- Permanent felt pens
- Patterned fabric • Buttons
- Soft-toy filling

1 Cut out a piece of white cotton fabric 18cm (7in) x 18cm (7in).

First draw a pillow-doll picture on paper.

Copy or trace your image onto the fabric.

2 Cut a piece of patterned fabric the same size as the white cotton square.

Pin the two pieces together, right sides facing.

Using backstitch, sew all the way around, 15mm (⅝in) away from the fabric edge. Leave a gap at the bottom.

3 Turn the pillow right sides out.

Fill up the pillow, fold the edges in and sew them together neatly.

4 Colour in the pillow and add buttons, if you wish, for decoration.

This view shows their plump pillow shape and pretty backing fabric.

Handy dolls

Create helpful hideaways

These dolls will make handy covers for your scissors. They also look pretty as key rings.

Trace the outline of this template onto tracing paper.

1 Cut out the template and pin it to the felt.

Cut out two body shapes.

Cut out any other felt shapes you're using.

2 Complete the front first.

Sew all your felt shapes to the front piece only, using running stitch.

3 Pin on the back and sew around the shape.

Leave a small gap in the stitches to allow room for the ribbon.

Overstitch the ends to stop the felt pieces coming apart.

4 Fold the ribbon in half. Bring the folded end through the scissors. Pass the ends of the ribbon though the loop and pull tight.

5 Attach a safety pin through the two ends of the ribbon.

6 Push the safety pin through the gap in the sitching from the inside.

7 Undo the pin and knot the ribbon ends.

Hideaway

To make your scissors disappear, pull the ribbon up so they go into the doll. To make them reappear, move the doll up the ribbon till the scissors are revealed.

Alien

Flower girl

Jolly pirate

For the body template, see page 106.

Handy features

Trace over these shapes to create the characters above. For the main part of the body, use the template on the previous page.

Jolly pirate's hat

Jolly pirate's eyepatch and scarf

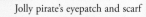

Robot

Super boy

What's hiding?

Check that the template is big enough to hide away your object. If you need to make it larger, try enlarging it on a photocopier.

Dolly in bed

Super boy's mask

Super boy's belt

Alien's eyes

Dolly in bed's flowers and bow

Robot's eyes and mouth

4

Knitting and sewing know-how

Creating dolls

For each project in this book, you'll find a list of everything you need to make it. The most essential piece of equipment is the sewing kit – have this ready at all times. Also shown here are some other things that you'll find useful.

Sewing kit

Here are the sewing essentials – keep them together in a handy box.

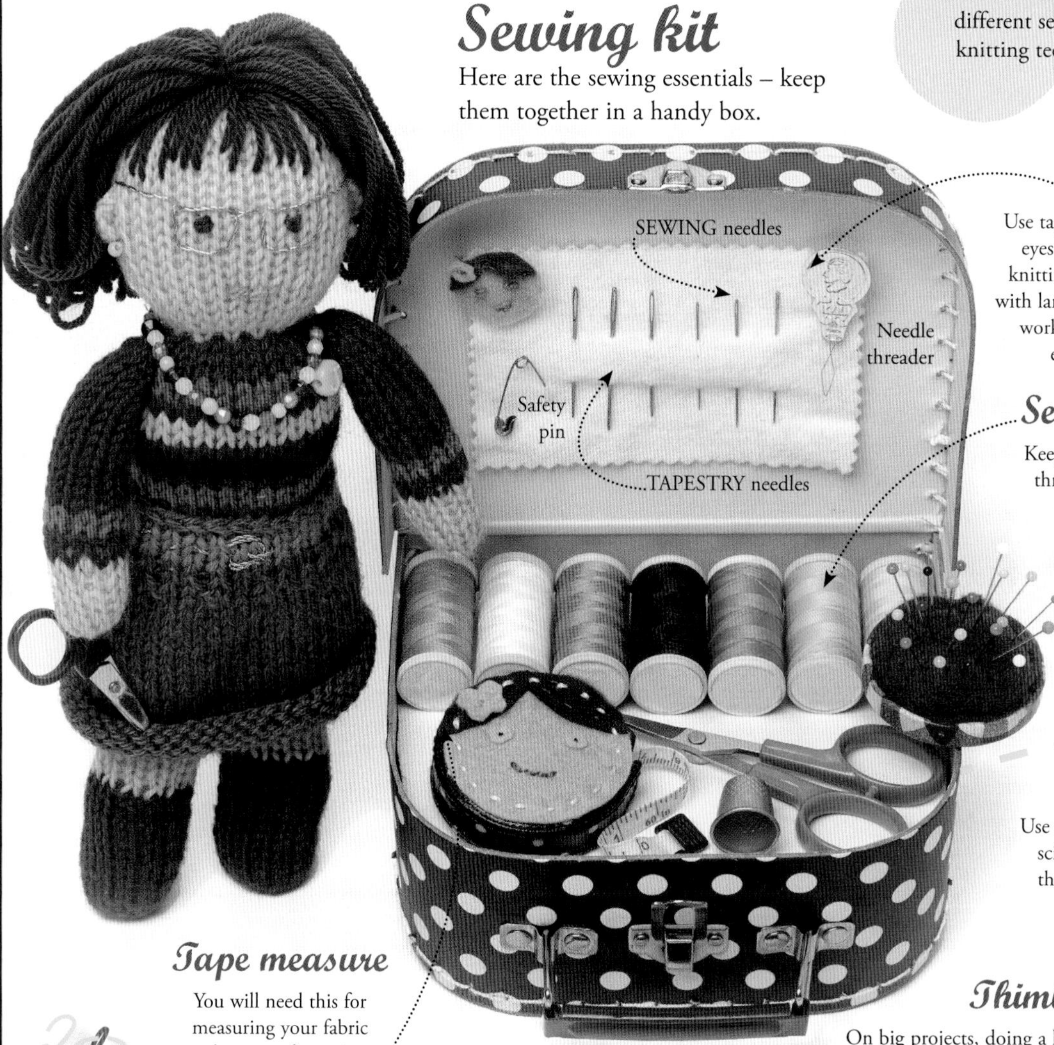

SEWING needles

Safety pin

TAPESTRY needles

Needle threader

Needles

Use tapestry needles with large eyes and rounded ends for knitting yarn. Sewing needles with large eyes and pointed ends work best with sewing and embroidery thread.

Sewing thread

Keep an array of colourful threads plus some other colours like black, grey and brown.

Pins

These are glass-headed dressmaking pins.

Scissors

Use small sharp embroidery scissors for snipping off threads and cutting out tiny doll shapes.

Tape measure

You will need this for measuring your fabric at the start of a project, and to help you position things accurately.

Thimble

On big projects, doing a lot of hand stitching can make your middle finger sore – use the thimble on this finger to push the needle through.

Ribbons

Ribbons work well for decoration. They are also useful for gathering fabric to make skirts and bags and for fastening clothes.

Felt fabric

Felt is very versatile. It's easy to shape and doesn't fray when you cut it – perfect for tiny projects like these shoes.

Soft-toy filling

This polyester fibre is used for all the projects in this book. It's very soft and can be worked easily into all the different doll shapes.

Embroidery thread

This thread is thick, so use it when you want to make stitches that show, or for stitches that are purely decorative.

Double knit (DK) yarn

Knitting needles 4mm (No6)

Knitting yarn and needles

All the knitting projects use Double knit yarn (DK) and size 4mm (No 6) knitting needles. How much yarn? Most projects are quite small, so it might be possible to use up your leftovers. To make it simple, each project refers to balls of yarn for each colour.

Stitch holder.

Large scissors

For cutting out templates and larger pieces of fabric, these scissors are ideal. Sharp scissors are easier to use than blunt ones and give the best results.

Pinking shears

These scissors will prevent cotton fabric fraying because their blades are zig-zag shaped. The effect is attractive as well and can be used for decoration.

How to stitch

Here are the stitches that are used for the projects. They all have a different job to do when you are joining fabric together for cushions, bags, and patchwork pieces.

How to start and finish

Begin stitching with a knot at the end of the thread. To end a row of stitches, make a tiny stitch, but do not pull it tight. Bring the thread back up through the loop and pull tight. Do this once more in the same spot, then cut the thread.

Running stitch

This is a very versatile stitch used for seams, joining fabric together, and gathering.

Keep the stitches and the spaces between them small and even.

Backstitch

This is the strongest stitch. It makes a continuous line of stitches so it is best for joining two pieces of fabric securely, such as the sides of a bag.

Make the stitch then bring the needle back to the place where the last stitch is finished.

VIEW FROM REVERSE

Bring the needle out ready to begin the next stitch.

Tacking stitch

This is a temporary stitch. It will be removed but it is useful for holding pieces of fabric in place before you sew them together properly. It is also known as a basting stitch.

Tacking stitches are like running stitches but are larger and don't need to be even.

Overstitch

These are tiny, neat, and even stitches that are almost invisible. Use them to top sew two finished edges together, such as when you are joining patchwork pieces.

Insert the needle diagonally from the back of the fabric.

Pick up only two or three threads of fabric.

Slip stitch

Use slip stitch when you want the stitches to be invisible. This stitch is made by slipping the thread under a fold of fabric. It is often used to join two folded edges, such as the openings of cushions.

Slide the needle into the fold of the fabric.

Bring the needle out then slide the needle in the other side.

Lazy daisy stitch

This pretty stitch is very useful for embroidery decoration. Draw out your daisy design first in light pencil, then follow the lines with your stitches.

1 Tie a knot in your thread and pull it up through the beginning of a petal and down at the end.

2 Now bring it up through another petal until you have finished the flower.

Chain stitch

This is a very useful decorating stitch – great for flower stems and leaves. You may need to practise the stitch to get it just right.

1 Tie a knot in the thread and pull it up through the fabric.

2 Now push the needle back down next to the thread.

3 Don't pull it tight, leave a little loop.

4 Now bring the needle up through the loop and pull the thread through.

5 Repeat stages 1 to 4, keeping the stitches as even as possible.

Practise chain stitch on a curved line so you can make shapes.

Blanket stitch

This stitch is good for making neat, decorative edges and for sewing one piece of fabric to another.

1 Tie a knot in the thread and pull the needle up through the fabric.

2 Push the needle back through next to the stitch and up below it, making sure the loose end is caught as shown.

3 Push the needle down and up again so it is the same size as the previous stitch, catching the loose thread again.

4 Repeat these steps to make more loops.

Cross stitch

You can make whole pictures using cross stitch.

1 Draw out crosses in light pencil on your fabric.

2 Sew a line of crosses from left to right in one direction...

... then finish them off by sewing back the other way.

Finishing off

On the back of the fabric, push the needle through the loop of the last stitch.

Pull the thread tight and repeat to make it secure.

Stitching tip

Try to keep your stitches neat and even.

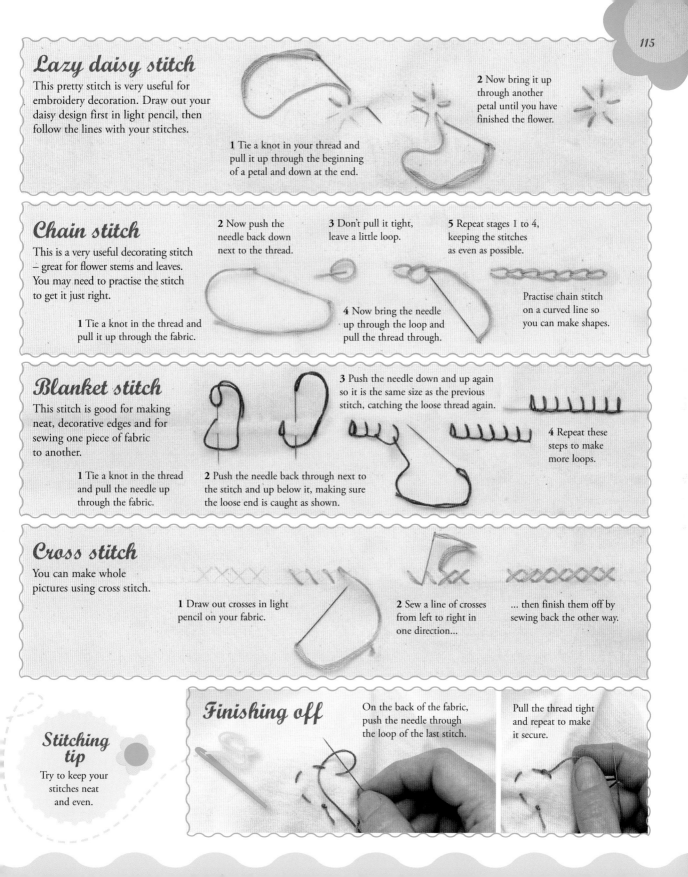

Loops, called stitches

Rows

Ball of yarn

How to knit

From casting on to casting off, whether you are just learning or already have the knitting know-how, these pages are a handy reference.

Slip knot
The first stitch on the needle is knotted so the yarn stays on.

Pull the ends of the yarn tight – now you have the first stitch.

Take a ball of yarn and make a loop at the end.

Bring the yarn through the loop to create a new loop.

Keep pulling the new loop through.

Attach the new loop to the needle.

Casting on
There are many ways to cast on. This method uses the thumb.

Wrap the yarn around your thumb as shown.

Pick up the yarn with the needle.

Let the yarn go from your thumb onto the needle.

Continue doing this...

... until you have enough stitches.

Joining new yarn

Do this when adding a new ball of yarn or making stripes.

2 Slide the knot up the yarn to the needle.

1 Tie the new yarn to the old yarn with a loose knot.

3 Continue knitting as usual.

Knit in a new colour

Here the knitting is shown on the reverse side. Join the new yarn as shown (left). To tidy up the loose ends of both colours, gather them up with the working yarn as you knit.

Stitches 1 2 3 4 5...

How many?

The projects in this book tell you how many stitches to cast on. Lots of stitches give you a wide fabric, while few stitches make a narrow fabric.

When you are starting a new row, begin with the first stitch on the right and work towards the left.

The yarn will be on the right as well.

Getting started

You will need to cast on the number of stitches required in the pattern. The stitches that are being worked will be on the left-hand needle, and the ones you have made will go on the right.

Casting off

Begin the row by knitting two stitches.

Pick up the first stitch with the left needle.

Carry this first stitch over the second stitch and over the end of the needle.

Repeat steps 1–3...

... until one stitch remains. Open up the loop

Cut the yarn and place the end in the loop.

Pull the yarn to close the loop.

Tidy away ends

Sew in the loose ends when adding new yarn or tidying the loose ends of finished pieces.

Use this method when tidying joined yarn or knitting stripes.

Thread the end with a tapestry needle.

Sew the thread into the edge of the knitting.

Bring the needle out and cut the yarn.

Use this method when tidying loose ends of finished pieces.

Thread the needle onto the loose end and sew down the side of the knitting.

Bring the needle out and cut the yarn.

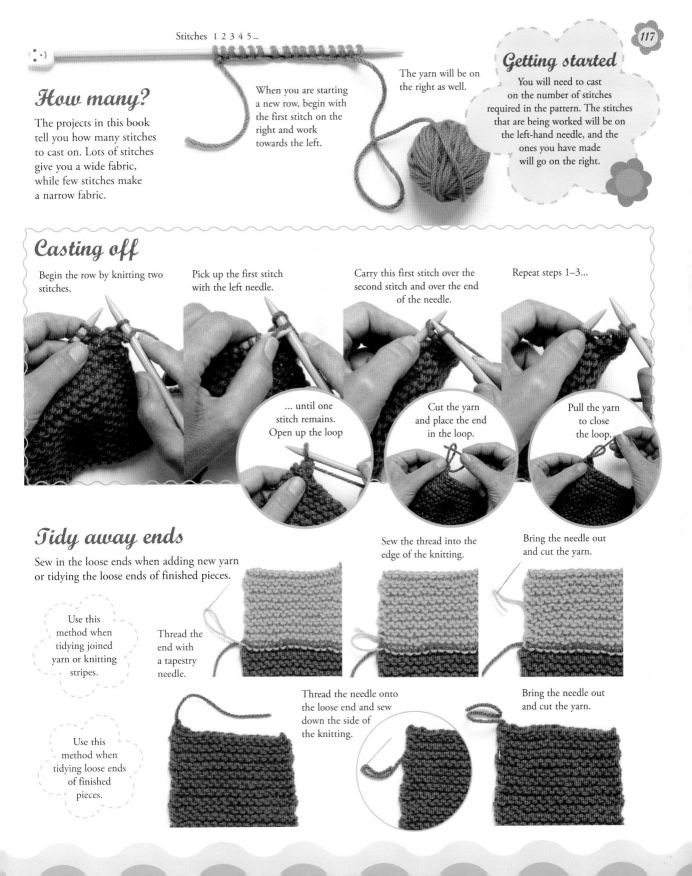

Knit stitch

Another name for knit stitch is plain stitch. Simple to make and regularly used in many projects, it is the most common stitch.

Method 1

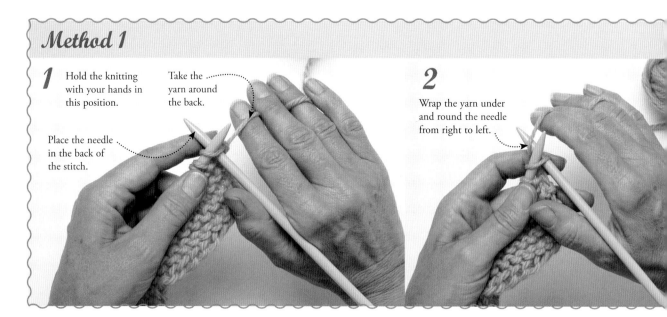

1 Hold the knitting with your hands in this position.

Take the yarn around the back.

Place the needle in the back of the stitch.

2 Wrap the yarn under and round the needle from right to left.

Method 2 This method might be helpful for left-handers.

1 Place the yarn between the fingers of your left hand.

2 Use your left index finger to move the yarn.

Place right needle into the stitch.

You can also make garter stitch if you knit every row in purl stitch.

Garter Stitch

Garter stitch isn't an actual stitch but the name given to a piece of knitting where every row is knitted in knit stitch. The effect is bobbly on both sides.

3 Pull on the yarn and move the needle from the back to the front.

4 The right needle is now on top of the left one and has taken the stitch with it.

5 Slide the top needle to the right. The stitch will now be transferred onto the right needle, completing the stitch.

Begin the next stitch as in step 1.

3 Bring the yarn down firmly between the needles.

4 Bring the needle with the loop of yarn to the front.

5 Take the needle with the stitch off the left-hand needle.

Begin the next stitch as in step 1.

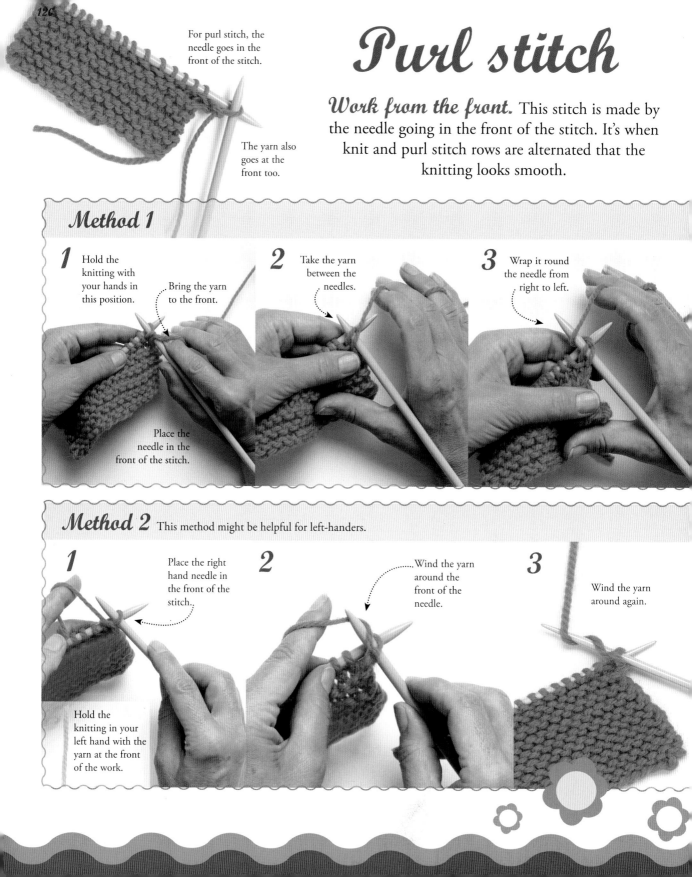

For purl stitch, the needle goes in the front of the stitch.

The yarn also goes at the front too.

Purl stitch

Work from the front. This stitch is made by the needle going in the front of the stitch. It's when knit and purl stitch rows are alternated that the knitting looks smooth.

Method 1

1 Hold the knitting with your hands in this position.

Bring the yarn to the front.

Place the needle in the front of the stitch.

2 Take the yarn between the needles.

3 Wrap it round the needle from right to left.

Method 2 This method might be helpful for left-handers.

1 Place the right hand needle in the front of the stitch.

Hold the knitting in your left hand with the yarn at the front of the work.

2 Wind the yarn around the front of the needle.

3 Wind the yarn around again.

Purl stitch + Knit stitch = Stocking stitch

Stocking stitch isn't an actual stitch at all. Instead it is made by working a knit row then a purl row, a knit row then a purl row and so on. The result is a smooth front to the knitting and a "bobbly" back.

BACK
The purl-stitch side

FRONT
The knit-stitch side

4 Pull on the yarn and move the needle from front to back ...

5 ...taking the stitch with it.

6 Take the rest of the yarn off the needle to complete the stitch.

Begin the next stitch as in step 1.

4 Bring the right hand needle from front to back taking the yarn with it.

5 Pull the rest of the stitch off the needle.

6 Now you are ready to begin the next stitch, starting at step 1 again.

Threading needles

NEEDLE TYPES

Tapestry needle   Sewing needle

Large eye,   Small eye,
rounded end   pointed end

THREADING EMBROIDERY THREAD OR WOOLLEN YARN

1 Loop the thread over a tapestry needle, pull tight, and remove the needle.

Keep the looped yarn pinched tight between your finger and thumb.

2 Bring the eye of the needle over the top of the yarn.

3 Pull the loop of yarn though the eye of the needle.

USING A NEEDLE THREADER

1 Push the threader wire through the eye of the sewing needle.

Put the end of the thread though the wire.

2 Pull the wire and thread through the eye.

3 Remove the wire.

Handy tip

If you work with thread that is too long it will get tangled, slowing you down. Cut a piece of thread roughly the length from your fingertips to your elbow.

Sewing on a button

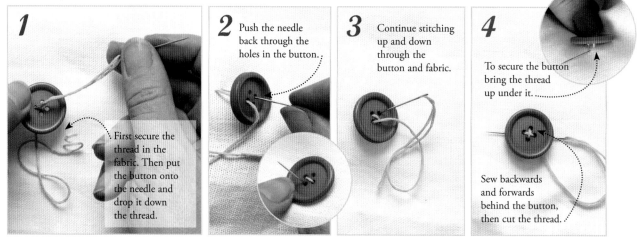

1 First secure the thread in the fabric. Then put the button onto the needle and drop it down the thread.

2 Push the needle back through the holes in the button.

3 Continue stitching up and down through the button and fabric.

4 To secure the button bring the thread up under it.

Sew backwards and forwards behind the button, then cut the thread.

Crochet chain stitch

Use this method to make the handles for the bags on page 70.

Please refer to page 116 to see how to make a loop.

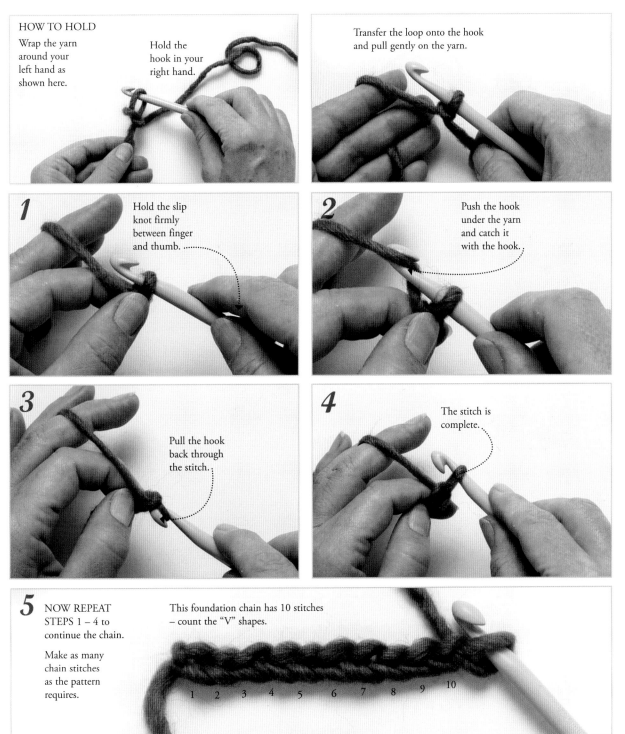

HOW TO HOLD
Wrap the yarn around your left hand as shown here.

Hold the hook in your right hand.

Transfer the loop onto the hook and pull gently on the yarn.

1 Hold the slip knot firmly between finger and thumb. ......

2 Push the hook under the yarn and catch it with the hook.

3 Pull the hook back through the stitch.

4 The stitch is complete.

5 NOW REPEAT STEPS 1 – 4 to continue the chain.

Make as many chain stitches as the pattern requires.

This foundation chain has 10 stitches – count the "V" shapes.

1 2 3 4 5 6 7 8 9 10

Index

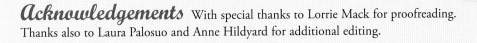

Acknowledgements With special thanks to Lorrie Mack for proofreading. Thanks also to Laura Palosuo and Anne Hildyard for additional editing.